Joe –

Best of success
during all your
negotiations

Bill Healy

Making Deals
The Business of Negotiating

Marvin Gottlieb

William J. Healy

New York Institute of Finance

Library of Congress Cataloging-in-Publication Data

Gottlieb, Marvin.
  Making deals : the business of negotiating / Marvin Gottlieb and William J. Healy.
    p.   cm.
  ISBN 0-13-552290-0
  1. Negotiation in business. I. Healy, William J. II. Title.
HD58.6.G67   1990   90-5762
658.4—dc20   CIP

Printed in the United States of America

10 9 8 7 6 5 4 3 2 1

New York Institute of Finance
2 Broadway
New York, New York, 10004-2207

To the best two deals ever to come my way; my wife Gail and my son Aaron.

M.G.

To Pat, my wife; Megan, Bryan, and Brett, our children; and my parents; for their years of support, belief, and encouragement.

W.J.H.

Contents

Acknowledgments

We would like to thank the many people who contributed to the development of this book. By sharing with us their time and insights, they were all instrumental in focusing our attention on real issues in negotiation. In particular, we would like to mention Harry Koenig, Morton Minkus, and David Whetton, for providing us the most important commodity of all—their experience.

Introduction

The place: Guatemala. There I am, cooling myself in the shade of a crowded clump of trees as the heat of the midday sun and the thickness of the jungle press on all sides. A small compound of hastily built, thatched, boothlike structures are arranged in a row. Around these structures, intense human interaction is taking place. What's happening here? Is it the creation of a rebellion? Will it affect the future of Central America? "How much—*cuanto?*" a voice barks. "150" is the reply. I am consulted, "What do you think?" I remain impassive, noncommittal. There is momentary silence. "What would I offer?" I think to myself. My confidant blurts, "100!" My heart sinks. "110," is the response. "O.K." A deal is struck. Is it a good deal? I'm not so sure. I imagine the look on my face resembling a cartoon character who has just sat on a wet chair. I am not happy. Is it that I am concerned about how history will portray this moment and my role in it? No. I just don't think we needed to pay 110.

Having gathered up the quilt she just purchased, and moved a small distance from the activity of the small Guatemalan market, my wife detects my displeasure. "Do you think it was too much?" she asks. "I think we could have got it for less," I say, not really answering the question. "You left me no room to bargain as soon as you said 100." "What should I have said?" she replies, a note of defensiveness creeping into her tone. I pause for reflection. Years of dealing with this "customer" had taught me that the fate of the remainder of my vacation could depend on my next response. I shift strategy. "Actually, it's a wonderful bargain even at 110." I go on to point out that it is only about $50 American. We spend a few moments discussing how well it will look here or there . . . and then, I get back to my point with my now more receptive audience. "When you offered 100, we were locked into a narrow bargaining range. I think he would have taken less—particularly since he split the difference in our favor. He was happy with the deal. I'm happy with the purchase, but I'm not happy with the deal."

I guess I'm currently too sensitive to these things, but negotiation has become a fixation for me. For the last several months, Bill and I have been thinking and breathing "negotiation." We have absorbed everything we can find that has been written on it, conducted focus groups, interviewed several deal makers in a variety of business settings, and have been presenting our findings to students and trainees in classrooms and seminar sessions. We're even in the process of writing a book on it.

My mind turns to a discussion Bill and I had before I left. We were grappling with a current trend in negotiation theory to force the process into a simple dichotomy. "I think it's useful to break down the concept of negotiation into parts," he offered, "but I'm not comfortable with the divisions we're using." "Maybe you're right," I reply, "but we need to get across that negotiation concerns much more than bottom line issues."

"Exactly! We are in agreement on that. It's just that the way we're doing it now seems inadequate to describe the complexity of what takes place in negotiation. Call it ego, self-esteem, or anything else, but a person has to walk away from a negotiation feeling good about the substantive issues, about one's relationship with the other negotiator, and about one's self separate from the relationship. I've told you about my house deal. . . ."

I was going to say, "Many times," but Bill was on a roll and he was making a good point.

"I considered all the market factors," he continued, "and I calculated what would be a very good price to begin bargaining with. When I stated my price position, the buyer said, 'Fine, I'll take it.' Had he not done that, I would have settled for less. But, worse than that, I was now unhappy with the deal I made even though it represented the best possible situation I had projected."

"I don't think you can guard against that happening once in a while . . ." I responded. "I have had similar experiences. As part of your preparation for negotiating—part of your planning process—you must take into account what you need to take away from the table on a personal or emotional level as well as the substantive side and the relationship-building issues. I can also see an advantage in speculating on what the other party has to take away in order to feel good."

"Right. Sometimes the dynamics of negotiation are more important than the result. For example, in a complex or multi-issue negotiation, the interaction leading up to gaining or yielding a point will have a significant impact on subsequent points depending on how the parties feel. If you give in too easily, even though I got what I wanted, I feel as though I've been had."

And, in fact, that was what I was feeling as I stood in the jungle with my newly purchased quilt.

PART ONE

Deal Making:
The Perspective

We are all deal makers. Whether in business, or in our personal lives, we buy, we sell, we barter for goods and services, for better relationships, for peace of mind. Our lives are full of dealings with vendors, bosses, subordinates, spouses, and children. We make deals with each other, with ourselves and, some of us, even in our prayers to God.

The five chapters in Part One provide a perspective—a background against which the techniques and strategies of the later chapters can be practiced. Chapter 1 provides an overview of the issues to be discussed in this book. Chapter 2 focuses our attention on the historical effects of negotiation and how this has affected current trends. Chapter 3 outlines the basic strategic issues involved in negotiation as a communication process. Chapter 4 examines the role of tactics as a means through which some negotiators attempt to gain an advantage. Finally, Chapter 5 delves into the issue of "style" and its effect on the way we negotiate.

These chapters relate to negotiation in a generic sense. That is, they present principles and observations that are relevant to any and all negotiation situations you may encounter.

CHAPTER 1

Making Deals

The lawyer for the buyer put down his coffee cup after assessing that the content was too cold to drink. He stretched back in his chair and said in a half yawn, "Look, we have been at this for two days, and I don't know about the rest of you, but I have a plane to catch in about two hours."

George was thinking, "We all have planes to catch. Why bring that up now? And, why is it always the guy who has the least to lose who puts on the pressure?" He glanced toward the end of the table where Stanley, his potential buyer, appeared engrossed in some minutiae of the proposed sale contract. Finally, he countered, "well, I think we're pretty close. . . ." He looked for confirmation from his lawyer, who also appeared deeply held by the significance of a comma on the page, since his eyes were not moving. Once again, George found himself thinking, "Where did I lose control of this? Things were moving along so well."

Things did seem to be moving along well. Five years ago when he opened the Florida branch it seemed like a great idea. Business was good, and several of his major customers were located in the south, with three in the Miami area. Besides, George and his wife had taken a liking to Florida, and he saw this as an opportunity to combine business with pleasure and a write-off. It had worked out nicely—at least on the business side. Even though the costs of shipping materials to the site were high, he covered it with the lower shipping costs to the regional customers. His major problem was with the labor force. His Florida workers exhibited—to his mind—a totally different work ethic than he was used to seeing in Allentown, Pennsylvania. In addition, there was the language problem. He had to have Spanish-speaking supervisors, and he was never sure that he was communicating effectively with them. Problems with order errors and quality control kept him much closer to the Florida operation than he had planned to be. It also meant that when he was in Florida, he was working and his family was beaching it alone. "Enough!" he had said after another in a series of arguments with his wife, and he put the business on the market.

"It seems to me," he began, trying to control his tone, "that we have been over everything a hundred times. Why can't we just sign this deal and be done with it?" He looked at Stanley, who remained inscrutable. "What's the problem?"

Stanley looked up from the contract, "Well, George, I sure would like to close this deal today so we can all go home to our families and forget about it, but. . . ."

"But what?" George retorted, almost in falsetto.

"The price."

"The price?! I thought we agreed on the price. All of the other concessions I've made in the contract have been predicated on that price. You never raised any issue about the price."

"Come on, George, you didn't think Stanley was going to pay your asking price." The voice belonged to Stanley's lawyer, who was now beginning to put things into his briefcase. "We figure you're about 20 percent over market. What's the real number you're after?"

George leaned back in his chair. He looked over at his lawyer, who cleared his throat, and then finally said, "We've thrown in a lot of stuff. You've got to admit that we've been generous."

"Generosity is not the issue," Stanley snapped, "that price is out of line. If I thought you were going to hang with that number I wouldn't even be here."

"All right Stan," his lawyer said while laying his ballpoint pen down on the table after clicking it into the writing position, "let's be fair. After all, they threw in the trucks, and that is a big plus. Can you live with a 15 percent markdown on the asking price rather than the full 20 percent?"

"I really wasn't prepared to go that high . . . but if it will close the deal. . . ."

What happened to George in this scenario probably wouldn't happen to you. Yet, many of the things that confound George in the process of trying to make a deal appear to happen in deal making everywhere. No deal is too large or too small to be subject to the kinds of problems present here, as well as many others yet to be introduced. In order to be an effective negotiator, you need to have some perspective on business negotiation in the real world.

Negotiation has always been one of the primary behavioral elements of human relationships, but rather than playing a cameo role in the background, it has taken a prominent place in our everyday lives. Whether the situation is business related, domestic, diplomatic, or psychological, most of us are finding negotiation to be an important component of personal, family, and business life. The fact is, we probably live in the most competitive era in history. We compete for attention with clients, among coworkers, socially, in our families and communities, and sometimes within ourselves. With so many separate influences angling for a piece of everyone's time, attention, and money, our ability to negotiate provides a critical competitive edge.

As with most efforts, how we function within the framework of negotiation is largely determined by our concept of what it is—or what we believe we are expected to accomplish. The term itself comes from the Latin, *negotiari*, to carry on business. Webster provides us with this useful definition, "To hold conference and discussion with a view to reaching agreement on a treaty, league, contract, etc.; to treat with another or others respecting peace, commerce, or any subject of *common concern*."[1] This definition is a good place to begin because it incorporates some of the basic principles built into this book.

First, to be effective as negotiators, we must see the process as a "conference" rather than a "contest" or "confrontation." We must operate with the objective of "reaching agreement," rather than "triumph." And we must approach negotiation from the perspective of "common concern" rather than "selfish demand." (Unfortunately, not everyone approaches negotiation with this conceptual framework.)

Many of you have given a great deal of thought to the issue of negotiation already. Some of you have attended workshops on the subject, and all of you have experienced at least some success or failure with your negotiations before picking up this book. If the book is successful in its objective to help you become better negotiators, it will be through building on your present knowledge, skill, and perception; the development of some new ideas, the application of tested principles, and the sharing of negotiation experience—your experience and the experience of others—in selling products, making deals, providing services, and generally finding your way through the hazards of the marketplace.

While there is much that is good in existing books and programs on negotiation, there are also some drawbacks. Most of the best known books and programs were conceived and built from the experience of a previous generation. Even though they attempt to adapt to the more current "win-win" jargon, they are based on an adversarial model. The underpinnings of these programs use a game-theory approach. This is contrary to a win-win outcome because in a game someone wins and someone loses.

One guiding principle this book follows is that "winning" means satisfying your substantive objectives without necessarily defeating the other negotiator, especially in long-term relationships.

Reaching a mutually satisfactory agreement is the best long-term outcome of a business negotiation—or any negotiation for that matter. Achieving this objective is best facilitated through a problem-solving approach. When people meet over a matter of common concern, a game model doesn't work. It is more productive to see negotiation as a problem-solving process.

The use of a problem-solving model changes the nature of the encounter. In problem solving, individuals convene for the purpose of finding answers, solutions, or comfort; problem-solving approaches provide the maximum opportunity for all of the participants to achieve their separate objectives.

This book presents negotiation as a business problem-solving process. It draws on research and practical experience with other problem-solving structures like conflict resolution and arbitration techniques.

Perhaps the key question is, how do we accomplish all that is necessary within a workable framework? The answer begins with the proper mindset. The effective negotiator is not adversarial, yet he or she undoubtedly has potentially different interests in the outcome. It is the concern for the substantive issues that sometimes obscures the other, perhaps equally or more important, issue—the relationship with the other side. Developing the proper mindset involves broadening your perspective to incorporate, in a very detailed way, the perspective of the other negotiator (purchasing agent, chief financial officer, management committee, travel manager, etc.).

An understanding of the substantive interests on the other side of the table will allow you to see the important issues clearly, and will identify sources of real and potential conflict. Since both parties are looking for the same outcome—an agreement they can live with— these issues can be redefined as a problem for both parties to solve, rather than as barriers to be overcome.

There are many difficulties associated with negotiation even though it takes place every day for each of us in different ways. Negotiation is in a transitional period. The old, or "classical," approaches using hard positional bargaining strategies are giving way to more collaborative approaches. However, the basic purpose remains the same—to resolve conflict over specific issues.

Any research into the whys and wherefores of everyday business and personal applications of negotiation, soon brings a realization of how much money inadequate negotiation skill could cost the average person over the course of a lifetime. Many people believe they are negotiating for the first time when they buy their first car or first home or some other large ticket item. In reality, everything we have acquired and many of the things that we have done throughout our lives have presented unknown and unrecognized opportunities in which we could have negotiated better deals for ourselves.

Everything we would want on a personal or business level is currently controlled, managed, owned, or protected by someone else. The difficulty that we face is how to get what we want (and frequently what we need) under the best circumstances, terms, price, and delivery possible.

The "best circumstances" under which we satisfy our needs for products, services, recreation, social ties, and other tangibles and intangibles is truly in the eyes of the negotiators. Two negotiators often view the same situation in radically different ways. A simple but familiar example is the acquisition of Manhattan island by the colonists. Who got the better deal? On the one hand, we can view this transaction as a screwing for the Indians. On the other hand, from the perspective of the Indians, who could not foresee the radical changes coming in their lives or their economy, the acquisition of valuable beads in trade for a relatively small and unneeded piece of land was an excellent deal.

It is unfortunate that we couldn't have been there to hear the negotiation. How did it begin? Had the settlers started bargaining for all of Manhattan island, Long Island, and parts of New Jersey? Did they get what they wanted? Or, did they have to settle for Manhattan in the face of hard bargaining from the Indian contingent? Were some beads withheld? Or, did the Indians get them all? This classic negotiation demonstrates some of the key negotiation elements covered in this book: information, power, time, and context.

Current trends in negotiation will be examined, showing how the old adversarial approaches are being abandoned for more problem-centered approaches in business, diplomacy, and even on the domestic front. Negotiation is perceived as a psychosocial phenomenon and as a problem-solving exercise. As interpersonal communication, negotiation is aligned with interview and conflict resolution techniques.

Third-party intervention and arbitration have become important parts of the negotiation landscape. Arbitration has initiated a great deal of research centering on the examination of business negotiation issues. As evidence of this, the American Arbitration Association has experienced extraordinary growth in the past five years.

While this general overview is very important to develop the proper negotiation mindset, the book is primarily concerned with the specifics in negotiation: tactics, planning, handling details, and style. Studies conducted by the authors have determined that to be an effective negotiator you must be aware of tactics and how to counteract them. In the perfect world, we would all be problem solvers, and tactics wouldn't be necessary. We don't advocate the use of tactics except as a countermeasure, but you cannot be sure that your fellow negotiator is approaching the situation with the same problem-solving spirit that you are. A bit of vest pocket wisdom that is currently circulating states that the only true victims are children; all the rest of us are volunteers.

Anyone who negotiates for a living quickly discovers that regardless of what else is going on in a negotiation, there is no substitute for sound planning. It is the nature of negotiation as a communication event to stimulate off-the-cuff responses and decisions which often are sorely regretted later on.

At a later point, this book talks about knowledge as a significant and powerful factor in negotiation. Knowing the details of your needs, trying to think like the other side, taking a broader view of events and circumstances outside of the negotiation that could influence the outcome, all play a part in the skilled negotiator's role.

Perhaps nothing influences the relationship side of negotiation more than the application of style used by the negotiators. While this manuscript was being prepared, the workers at Eastern Airlines were conducting a bitter strike—essentially against the style of Frank Lorenzo, the company president and chief executive officer. Thus far, thousands of travelers have been inconvenienced, thousands of workers have gone without pay checks, a significant portion of the work force will probably never regain their jobs, and an attempt to purchase the company has been scrapped, all because the relationship between labor and management is so poor.

We all have a prevailing style of negotiating that is part of our general way of dealing with conflict. The skilled negotiator is able to work around his or her prevailing style, and adapt to the style appropriate for the situation.

There are six key areas or focus points developed in this book that, when mastered, can significantly improve your ability to put together better deals.

1. Identifying and initiating a deal;
2. Planning a deal;
3. Identifying the negotiation ranges of a deal;
4. Analyzing the factors which influence the outcome of a deal;
5. Resolving conflicting issues in a deal; and
6. Adopting an effective style to build a relationship with those on the other side of the deal.

Perhaps one of the greatest pitfalls in negotiation is failing to perceive the opportunity to negotiate. Becoming a skilled negotiator means constantly working toward an increasing awareness of negotiable situations and issues. It also means viewing negotiation as a structured process with a natural progression which has specific rules in procedure and communication.

While there are many exceptions, the following stages typify the life of a negotiation.

1. *Identify and Plan.* Select and target appropriate situations for negotiation. Establish the game plan for entering negotiation: background, research, pricing, historical precedence, market and industry trends, and any related company or personal issues that could bear on the negotiation.

2. *Establish Contact.* The parties or intermediaries meet. Positions and issues are questioned, probed, and examined Deal ranges are established or estimated on the most critical issues.

3. *Present or Propose a Deal.* Based on the information concerning the needs, limits, personalities, styles, and other variables uncovered during the probing and questioning, one party presents a proposal for consideration by the other party.

4. *Conflict Resolution.* Differences are examined. Alternative solutions are considered and weighed against the substantive needs and the desire to build and maintain a working relationship.

5. *Confirmation and Action Plan.* Upon reaching a satisfactory resolution of differences, both parties confirm their understanding of all the terms of the deal—first verbally, then in writing (i.e., letter of agreement, contract, or lease). This should be facilitated quickly since the more time that elapses, the more memories fail and the more likely that circumstances will cause additional items to be brought into play. Although legitimate issues may arise following the signing of an agreement, these are better negotiated against the backdrop of an already completed deal.

Our opening scenario doesn't reveal exactly how George's deal was initiated. But we can see that he is a motivated seller. We might ask several questions about how this deal came to be. Who found Stanley? George's lawyer? Were there other suitors? Where are they now? What happened to the planning, the attention to detail? How did George get blind-sided? George allowed himself to be surprised about the price issue. It came late in the negotiation, after he had made serious concessions based on the assumption that price was not an issue.

Another question one might ask about George's deal is, "Who's side is his lawyer on?" Along with the other variables it is important to gain an understanding of the emphasis—both positive and negative—that third parties like lawyers, accountants, agents, and other advisors play in the deal-making arena.

Although George's deal did not involve international issues, one of his reasons for selling revolved around his problems with the cultural and linguistic orientation of the work force. In today's world of deal making, intercultural issues are often in full evidence if not predominant. Again, the skilled negotiator must be concerned with the special problems of international and intercultural negotiation. The intercultural elements add a dimension which is not encountered in other types of negotiation, but is critical to the success of international business.

The act of negotiation is at once positive, relationship building, and in line with a more professional approach to doing business. It is a problem-solving activity that allows the parties involved in a negotiation to satisfy their substantive interests in a mutually satisfactory way, while building or maintaining a good working relationship.

This problem-solving approach will make you a more effective negotiator whether or not the same methods are employed by the other side. However, there are many tricks and strategies that can still pop up and surprise the unwary.

If you are a salesperson, you understand the necessity of getting the best possible deal for the company, and that reaching agreement means closing the sale. On the surface, it might seem that good problem-solving negotiation and good selling are at odds with one another. This is not the case. Sales methodology is evolving also. Today, good salespeople are taking a much more consultative role in their selling practice. This consultative approach to selling is very compatible with the type of negotiation fostered in this book.

Negotiation is not a simple matter of give and take. As part of the human condition, it is tied to our self-esteem. Our success or failure to negotiate effectively relates directly to our feelings of self-worth. Some see it as a game and play to win. Some see it as threatening and avoid it because the potential for conflict is too unpleasant.

The authors have come to realize through experience and research that negotiation is an integral part of our interpersonal relations and should be viewed as a means to handle conflict, rather than as a game or a threat.

As with many things, the success of negotiation is best judged by the outcome. However, the manifestations of the outcome are not always obvious. In fact, the outcome is often judged subjectively rather than on hard objective criteria. Most of us have come to believe or at least parrot the phrase, win-win. Unfortunately, when businesspeople are questioned about the meaning of this phrase, their responses center around compromise. This book promotes the idea that good outcomes in negotiating are not compromises. More important, the concept of compromise actually gets in the way of good problem-solving negotiation.

The most successful negotiators are those that focus on questions and strategy rather than tactics; on testing the understanding of others' positions rather than obstinately defending their own, and on the feeling or psychosocial aspects of the interaction as well as the substance of the deal.

Notes

[1]*Webster's Third New International Dictionary of the English Language* (Springfield, MA: Merriam, 1966) p. 1514.

CHAPTER 2

Developing an Approach

People don't learn how to negotiate from books. In fact, by the time a person is old enough to read a book on negotiation, innumerable negotiated "deals," and some crucial ones at that, have already been made. Young children negotiate for trust and responsibility, teenagers negotiate for privileges, young adults negotiate for freedom of choice. Thus trying to say something important about negotiation is not like demonstrating macrame to someone who never tied anything more complicated than a shoelace.

This book is an "enhancement" of what most people already know either consciously or instinctively about negotiation. Compare negotiation training to learning how to run more effectively. Everyone runs. We can look at a person placing one foot in front of the other in rapid succession and say, "That person is running." However, anyone who has taken up running as a sport, or even for its aerobic benefits, soon learns that there is "running" and then there is *running*.

The trained runner makes many of the same moves as the untrained one. The moves made are the result of choice. The trained runner, much like the professional negotiator, is concerned with planning, preparing, pacing, and becoming familiar with the course to be traveled, the distance, the competition, and the finish line.

Since the focus of this discussion is on the negotiation of business-related issues, think about where and when people learn about negotiating these issues. For most of us, it probably wasn't until several years into our business careers that we were, in fact, exposed to a course or program in negotiating. Thinking back beyond that for the authors, in the over 30 years of higher education between us, there was never a formal course offered in the subject. The vast majority of us learn how to negotiate through trial and error and the observation and influence of others.

Negotiation as a mode of conflict resolution has been evolving along with other communication styles for centuries. This has been a slow evolution and, indeed, most of the stylistic changes have occurred at an accelerating rate during this century.

In viewing negotiations that have taken place during the last 40 years, we can see some definite shifts in emphasis (e.g., the rise in the use of tactics). Virtually every book on negotiation devotes several chapters to the examination of tactics and how to counter them. In more recent times, there have been some voices calling out for a less tactical, more problem-solving negotiation style. While we fit more in the latter category, we have tried to remain sensitive to the continuing predominance of tactics as a method among professional negotiators.

We also sense a shift away from compromise as an acceptable outcome of negotiation. *Recent research has pointed to the fact that compromise often plants very critical seeds for future discontent. In fact, compromise might be looked at as a settlement in which both parties sooner or later realize that they had neither their substantive or relationship needs satisfied—what we call a "lose-lose."*

A closer look at what occurred during the period 1975 to 1990 reveals some very interesting trends and raises some intriguing questions. What has been the impact of changes in the work ethic? What is the impact of the decline of labor unions? How about the impact of increased globalization of markets? The rate and ability to communicate faster and more efficiently? The increasing intercultural, personal, and business dealings? All of these things and many more have an effect on the way people resolve conflict, and, therefore, on how they negotiate.

Think of how this shift has occurred in your personal life. Do you find yourself negotiating things that only a short time ago seemingly existed without the need of negotiation? The U.S. Bureau of Labor Statistics tells us that 15 years ago about 40 percent of the work force was made up of women. Today that number is closing in on 60 percent. What new conflicts have had to be resolved—negotiated—because of families? Who does the dishes? Takes out the garbage? Takes care of the children? Who gets the bathroom first in the morning? Who takes off when illness strikes the children in the household?

In the end, a generally accepted equalization of roles has developed for husbands and wives. When a husband is offered a corporate relocation, the spouse does not necessarily drop her life and begin packing. Husbands have negotiated successfully with employers for paternity leave. What was once a hard position to negotiate—dictated by the "head of the household" and chief bread winner—has been tempered by the family's need for additional cash flow and the well-educated, career-oriented wife's need to continue her personal development.

These changes in traditional roles have given rise to a significant amount of negotiation taking place in everyone's personal life. This need to negotiate continually has accelerated interest in negotiation and has changed the way we do it.

Another trend that is easily noticed is the increasing use of third-party negotiators. Sports disputes, labor disputes, and business and civil legal issues are using more arbitration to accomplish out-of-court settlements.

Still another strong influence on negotiation is the increasing use of electronic tools to move information and calculate deal components that would have taken significantly more time (or in some cases, been impossible) just a short while ago. Changes in contracts that once were sent back and forth through the mail are now faxed for comment and approval while negotiation is conducted over phone lines across the country or the world.

The fact is that negotiation is a lifelong process that we begin learning as children. We receive very little formal training in negotiation throughout our lives, yet our ability to negotiate greatly affects our influence on others, and our very ability to succeed in a substantive way personally and professionally.

Throughout our lives we bargain with teachers, employers, clients, investors, associates, family members, and all providers of goods and services important to the substance and quality of our lives. Sometimes we know when we are negotiating, as when we are negotiating wages or the purchase of a piece of property. At other times, the process is so subtle, we may be unaware we are negotiating, as when a friend makes a dinner suggestion, or a child discusses the need for additional TV time.

THE CHANGING STYLE OF NEGOTIATION

You don't have to be a student of negotiation strategy to get a sense that the way people negotiate is changing. We are living in a world where the Soviet Union has taken the initiative to put mutual problem-solving proposals on the table relating to strategic arms reduction, Afghanistan, and trade relations. The Soviets have long been the primary example of hard positional bargaining characterized by the tactic of extreme demands. Here in America, employees now negotiate for ownership of the companies they work for, and share in both the profits and the problems of management.

However, in the same world, we are experiencing the rise of fundamentalism, and a particularly inflexible mode of bargaining that is tied to nationalism and religious fanaticism. Yet, even hostage situations sometimes yield to third-party arbitration.

RESOLVING CONFLICT

Negotiation is a conflict resolution activity. We have already said that a problem-centered, consultative approach is best. Although the outcomes can be much more complex, it is useful to focus on three possibilities as a way of underlining our point: Win-Lose, Lose-Lose, and No-Lose (often called win-win).

Win-Lose

When a negotiation is resolved in a win-lose, one party gets what he wants while the other side goes away feeling that he came up short. Win-lose strategies have been analyzed extensively, beginning with von Neumann and Morgenstern's book, *Theory of Games and Economic Behavior*.[1]

Although primarily a tool for research in classical economics, game theory commanded the attention of bargainers and researchers in negotiating strategies for several decades. Game theory assumed that (1) bargainers were rational and could calculate the best outcome from available information, (2) the rules of the game were known in advance and remained fixed throughout the game, (3) each player had perfect knowledge of alternative outcomes and values attached to these outcomes, (4) contextual and outside influences did not affect the model, and (5) perceptions and expectations remained fixed throughout the game.

These assumptions bore no resemblance to real life situations, and admittedly so. The value of game theory was its use as a benchmark for classifying and analyzing models of conflict.

By the mid-1960s, researchers acknowledged the shortcomings of game theory as a way of studying the negotiation process. First, there always had to be a winner and a loser. There was no alternative to account for those situations where both sides had their substantive needs satisfied as a result of bargaining, or changed their goals and aspirations as a result of communication and a better understanding of the problem causing the conflict.

The popularity (and durability) of win-lose as a strategy was confirmed by several studies done in the late 1970s based on direct observation of actual negotiations. In a 1978 study[2] it was concluded that successful negotiators maintain their enthusiasm throughout the session, rely on information gained in previous sessions, and use coercive strategies to restrict the freedom of their opponents.

Power is the primary force in win-lose negotiating. There is a great reliance on and projection of authority. But unlike a parent-child relationship or a supervisor-worker relationship, the locus of the power is not so well defined.

In the ideal situation, both negotiators have the same need to reach an agreement, such as a prospect who needs the products and services as badly as the salesperson wants to sell them. It is rare to find a prospect who wants the product more than you want to sell it. And yet, many prospects walk away from a negotiation feeling that they have gotten the short end. This results from a different kind of power, intellectual or mental power.

Win-lose is institutionalized in the democratic process itself. On one hand, the principle of majority rules, a win-lose construct, is almost universally admired. On the other hand, however equitable it may appear, it results in one group getting its way and another going away unsatisfied.

In their book, *Understanding Human Communication*, Adler and Rodman outline some circumstances when win-lose is the preferred outcome.

> There are some circumstances when the win-lose method may be necessary, as when there are truly scarce resources and where only one party can achieve satisfaction. For instance, if two suitors want to marry the same person, only one can succeed. And . . . it's often true that only one applicant can be hired for a job.[3]

Lose-Lose

When a lose-lose outcome occurs, neither party is satisfied. Strangely enough, this is a more common approach to conflict resolution than you might think. The most respectable form of this approach is *compromise*. In the typical compromise, both negotiators settle for less than they want because they believe it is the best result they can hope for.

Albert V. Filley, a noted researcher in conflict resolution, offers an interesting observation. He poses the question, "Why is it that if someone says, 'I will compromise my values,' we view the action unfavorably, yet we speak with admiration about parties in a conflict who compromise to reach a solution?"[4] While it is true that compromise may in fact be the best obtainable result in some negotiations, working together in a problem-solving context can often uncover much better solutions.

There are worse lose-lose results than compromise. In some instances where both parties are striving hard to be winners, the outcome of the struggle leaves them both losers.

No-Lose (Win-Win)

No-lose is the problem-solving approach to conflict resolution. The objective is finding solutions that satisfy everyone's needs. It begins with the basic mindset that, by working together, it's possible to reach goals on both sides without the need for compromise. Here are a couple of examples.

A warehouse operation for a major record company had a conflict with the warehouse workers over the scheduling of necessary overtime. While overtime pay is attractive, the employees didn't want to be locked into spur of the moment overtime calls. The feeling was that they couldn't make plans that would accommodate their personal and social needs. The warehouse supervisors needed to be sure that the operation was fully staffed at all times. After some discussion they arrived at a solution that satisfied everyone: The supervisors worked up a rotation list with all of the names in a particular department. As a worker's name came closer to the top of the list, that worker became eligible for the overtime call. Employees were free to trade hours among themselves as long as the operation was fully staffed as needed.

A husband and wife find themselves arguing frequently over their budget. The husband was a computer buff who enjoyed buying new software, while the wife feared these continual purchases would ruin her carefully constructed budget. Their solution was to set aside a small amount of money each month for such purchases. The amount was small enough to be affordable, yet gave the husband a chance to indulge in his hobby. In addition, the wife was satisfied with the arrangement since software was now a budget category by itself, which got rid of the "out of control" feeling that came when her husband made unexpected purchases.

The no-lose approach is a way of creatively finding unique answers to unique problems.

APPLYING PROBLEM SOLVING TO NEGOTIATION

Of the three possible outcomes, the no-lose approach is the most desirable for a negotiation. In order to achieve this outcome we need:

A noncompetitive attitude;

A clear understanding of needs/goals;

A special set of skills;

A certain amount of cooperation from the other negotiator.

Problems needing solutions are the driving force behind any negotiation. If there were no problems, we probably wouldn't be negotiating. This emphasis on the problem should govern your approach. It provides the motivational push you need to negotiate, and underscores the need for careful and detailed planning. The ability to clearly grasp your needs from a personal and organizational vantage point plays a key role in your problem-solving ability.

All parts of a negotiation are not problematic. Unless some unsavory strategies are being employed, there are always points of agreement. Problem solving occurs when there is conflict over needs—that is, your need and my need do not apparently yield to the same satisfier.

Begin each problem-solving sequence with a mirror statement that reflects back to the other party your understanding of their concerns. This helps clarify and confirm your understanding of the conflict. With the need and the disparity held out clearly before both parties, the task now becomes finding a way to resolve the conflict that would meet everyone's needs.

In a many types of negotiations, this is often done with more than one conflict on the table at a time, since the solution to one problem may lie in the modification of or solution to a different conflict. Once all of the scenarios are before the parties, they are evaluated individually and against one another. The result should be a decision, not a compromise.

Table 2.1 outlines the basic steps of the problem-solving component in a negotiation.

No-lose solutions are not always possible in negotiation or any other problem-solving arena. No matter how hard we try there will be times when, because of a variety of reasons, the situation will not yield to the complete application of problem-solving techniques. In those cases, there will be elements of compromise. But even then the preceding steps haven't been wasted.

The genuine desire to learn what the other person wants and your interest in trying to satisfy those desires will build a climate of good will. This can help you find the best solution to the present conflicts and build good relationships and strong bridges for future negotiations.

THE ARBITRATION OPTION

One of the changes we have seen in the evolution of conflict resolution is the increasing use of arbitration to settle differences. Primarily a tool for settling labor disputes, arbitration techniques and third-party mediation are finding increasing acceptance in disputes other than those concerning labor and management.

Table 2.1. Negotiating Steps

Prenegotiating
Take inventory of problems:
  Personal
  Organizational
Plan for the negotiation:
  Anticipate problems that may develop
  Gather, arrange, and organize all relevant information
  Examine alternative solutions

While Negotiating
Define the specific problem:
  Identify the need
  Isolate areas of conflict
  Establish criteria for evaluating potential solutions
  Assess mix of negotiating styles
Generate alternatives:
  Minimize restrictions and analysis while generating alternatives
  Examine current conflict in relation to other perceived conflicts
Evaluate the alternatives:
  Measure potential solutions against criteria
  Focus on meeting the need rather than modifying a position
Get an agreement:
  Select the alternative or combination of alternatives that best meet(s)
  the needs of both parties
  Reconfirm support for the solution on both sides

Although formal arbitration has some of the aspects of a trial or court hearing, there is less formality. An arbitrator will generally allow all evidence that relates to the issue to be presented, without the usual restrictions of a courtroom judge. Documents and other tangible evidence to support a position should be prepared very carefully, since they provide an important source for the arbitrator to base his or her decision.

Testimony is another important source of evidence. When a person is identified as an authority on the facts, he or she is generally allowed to testify without interruption. Witnesses in arbitration are subject to cross examination. This succeeds in bringing out facts that are not disclosed in direct testimony, correcting misstatements, placing facts in their true perspective, reconciling apparent contradictions, and attacking the reliability and credibility of the witness.

Robert Coulson, president of the American Arbitration Association, discusses some of the important reasons for not being restrictive about the presentation of evidence in his book *Labor Arbitration: What You Need To Know.*

> There are many reasons why technical evidentiary rules are not suitable in arbitration. First, arbitration is intended to be an informal procedure. Second, the rules of evidence are essentially rules of exclusion. They were developed to prevent a jury from hearing or considering prejudicial or unreliable testimony and exhibits. In arbitration, a sophisticated person, selected by the parties for technical knowledge and good judgment, hears the case; such a person should be able to disregard evidence that is not helpful, relevant, or reliable. Third, there may be a therapeutic value in allowing witnesses to vent their feelings or "get things off their chests," even if the testimony has little probative value. Finally, an award will not be overturned because of a liberal admission of evidence as long as the arbitrator does not base the award on obviously irrelevant or erroneous evidence. On the other hand, refusal to hear relevant evidence may constitute grounds for vacating the award.[5]

The reference to "getting things off their chests" is worth highlighting as a shared attribute of arbitration and negotiation. The best opportunities for no-lose outcomes occur in settings where both parties are open about their needs and about how they are reacting to the negotiation process itself. Skilled negotiators present themselves as flesh and blood human beings as well as the representatives of a particular point of view.

THE FOUR MAJOR VARIABLES

Conflict resolution techniques like problem solving and arbitration provide a framework for reaching satisfactory agreements. However, they are applied in an atmosphere that is charged with other significant variables. The driving forces behind most negotiations are time, information, power, and context.

Time

Time is rarely a neutral force in negotiation. It is either working for or against you. In nearly every case, when we negotiate, we do not have an unlimited amount of time. Depending on the circumstances, several sessions may be necessary to complete one negotiation; each session with its own time limit. However, we may negotiate from start to finish without ever leaving the room. But we are always conscious of time as a driver.

Deadlines. One or both parties may be working against a deadline. In fact, more problem-solving activity is generated in negotiation when there is a common deadline, since the deadline can be seen as an enemy that is greater than the other negotiator. In Chapter 8, we discuss the time factor in intercultural settings. Other cultures have a different attitude toward what constitutes a deadline. Sensitivity to the issues surrounding time is a very important negotiating trait.

It is best to avoid revealing anything to do with your own deadlines. However, always look for signs and signals regarding the other party's approaching deadlines:

The entrance of a new person into the negotiation;

A softening on a hard-line position;

A concession on an issue;

An increase in the pace of the events;

References to time occurring frequently in and out of context.

Time pressure can be created in a negotiation to encourage the process to move more quickly or to get through a deadlock:

Limited time offer;

Contingent offers for quick decisions;

Impending price increases;

Limited resources or supply of what they need.

The inherent danger in creating false deadlines is that a skilled negotiator is likely to disregard them, and if they are not adhered to, you lose credibility.

The Pareto Principle or 80/20 Rule[6] applies particularly well to deadlines in negotiation. Many experts feel that as much as 80 percent of the concessions in any given negotiation occur in less than the last 20 percent of the negotiating time. This builds a strong case for holding out your concessions until later in the process. A concession which may have little impact early in the negotiation can become the "sweetener" that closes the deal at the end.

When to Negotiate. There are many negotiation situations where you are in control of when to negotiate. Assuming no inordinate deadline, you are usually in control of when you buy and sell things. If you are a buyer for your company and you make repetitive purchases, you are probably sensitive to market factors that can drive the prices up or down depending on the timing of the purchase.

When negotiating a long-term contract, significant dollars can be saved (as much as 5 percent according to knowledgeable purchasing agents) if the purchase is made on the down side of a supplier's business cycle. Other purchases benefit from being negotiated at the end of a fiscal year, when the salesperson needs the deal to make a quota or a bonus.

In a buy-sell situation, it is the buyer who generally controls the timing by initiating the negotiation. On the selling side, the most important timing factor is delivery. If the seller can determine that the buyer has delivery pressure, he or she can negotiate the price up.

Information

Information has two specific components: (1) information about the variety of negotiating options or potential alternatives to meet your needs, and (2) information about the specific negotiation in which you are involved.

Information about the range of potential negotiating solutions is critical to enable you to avoid getting locked into a situation that you cannot walk away from. A simple example is the situation of the home buyer who wants a house in a particular area and must move in by September 1. It happens that in this area there is only one house for sale that meets the buyer's requirements. With no other options, and having to vacate the current house by the same date, the buyer is in a poor position to negotiate. A lack of information about other possibilities or options for satisfying your needs creates a single-issue bargaining climate—with price being the issue. You can't walk away from the deal, so be prepared to pay a steep price.

Another example is the salesperson who has been prospecting for business and discovers a company presenting an opportunity. It also happens that the salesperson needs to bring in additional business to make quota. An inordinate amount of time is spent with this particular prospect in the hope that a sale can be made. As time progresses, the salesperson begins to realize that this prospect is not as "hot" as was first thought. However, having limited one's options in regard to available prospects, the salesperson is in the position of having to grant concessions to get the business.

One way, then, of looking at information, is to see the necessity for gaining as much information as possible about options *outside* of the deal being considered. Ask, "If not this, then what?" And have an answer before you sit down to negotiate.

The second major impact of information occurs *inside* the deal. It has been said by professional negotiators that the party with the most information will come out best. The more information we have about the individual or individuals we are negotiating with, their personal needs, their organizational needs, their positions and interests, the better we will be able to react to and anticipate their negotiating requests. The results from several research interviews demonstrate that preparation is the key to successful negotiation.

While it is important to gather as much information as possible before a negotiation begins, gaining information during the negotiation is even more critical. Effective negotiators are masters of the art of asking fact-finding questions. The information being sought concerns data about what the other side really wants. There is a natural tendency in negotiation to be guarded about self-disclosure; however, we must ask questions and seek information beyond what the other side is willing to openly share with us. The more information we can gather through accurate and astute questioning, the better able we will be to size up their needs and issues. Understanding all of the *who, what, why, where, when, how,* and *to what extent* issues will help to identify hidden agendas and real needs.

In addition to asking factual questions, it is critical to get at the emotional issues or feelings that surround the negotiation. How does the outcome of the negotiation affect the other negotiator personally? How does it affect others? How do these emotional issues affect the way components of the deal are valued? An important key to negotiation success is the discovery of the relative value the other side places on the various issues and components of the deal.

When considering your need for information about a negotiation, think about all of the possible sources of information. Information can come from competitors, people who do business with the other side, trade reports or recent articles featuring the other side, or from standard references.

Many negotiations fail to achieve the desired outcome because of the lack of readily obtainable information. Whenever possible, ask the same questions of different people within an organization. If appropriate, have technical experts from your organization ask questions of technical experts within a target or prospect organization. Asking the same questions at different locations and levels within an organization can build a composite of information that is useful for discovering real issues, and is often more open and truthful than information you may receive from the person you are negotiating with. Needless to say, caution must be taken not to be perceived as inappropriately snooping around. However, obtaining the information may yield far more benefits than avoiding the risk of being thought of as a snoop.

Power

The ability to influence or direct the decisions and/or actions of the other side in negotiation is power. Power is also relative. There are very few instances in negotiation where one individual or party exercises complete control or dominance over the other side. In such cases, you would be giving orders, not negotiating. Power is often a function of perception. If I have power but you fail to see it, or react as if I don't have power, the advantage of my power is greatly diminished. Conversely, my actual power may be very low; however, I have built up a perception of power and, therefore, command more influence over the negotiation's outcome.

Power as an element of negotiation is very often misunderstood. We perceive the unequal match between a major corporation, a land baron, or a developer with seemingly endless resources of money, labor, and legal talent pitted against the small homeowner sitting on a corner lot required for a skyscraper or a shopping center. Yet, who has the power? The power rests with the side that can most easily walk away from the deal. Many a building has been constructed around a small house that wouldn't be moved.

Exercising power can be risky or costly and the exercise of too much power can irreparably damage business relationships. The balance of power can change significantly during the course of a negotiation or in subsequent negotiations. However, before entering a negotiation, you must assess the relative power of the parties involved. Among the sources of power we will consider are:

Risk,
Knowledge/information,

Expertise,

Reward/punishment,

Legitimate/positional,

Identification/association,

Referent/moral.

The existence of power in and of itself is not bad or wrong. The frequent objections that people have regarding power are: (1) someone else has it and we don't, (2) it is being used in a coercive, dominant, or manipulative way, and (3) a disagreement with the ultimate purpose for which the power is being used.

Risk Taking Power. Knowing who will suffer the greatest risk in a deadlock or no deal situation can be an important source of leverage. The ability to walk away from a deal provides a distinct negotiation advantage. If you can walk away without any great consequence to yourself or your constituents, you are in the driver's seat—assuming the other side cannot do the same.

In the vast majority of business negotiations, however, there are always consequences associated with walking away—for both sides. As part of the planning process, it is critical for each party entering the negotiation to consider carefully the consequences of a no-deal outcome. The age-old wisdom of looking for a loan (or a date) when you need one least, or shopping for new leases when you are not under any pressure to move can result in some of the most creative and worthwhile deals when compared with the deals that are struck when one party must reach an agreement before an approaching deadline.

Knowledge/Information Power. We have already discussed the necessity for comprehensive information in a negotiation to determine the real issues and find appropriate solutions. However, as Francis Bacon said, "Knowledge is power." The power of one's information rests in both the quantity and the quality of that information.

The amount and access to information available to negotiators has increased dramatically in the past few years, primarily as a result of advances in technology.

Also, the quality of the available information has been enhanced by improved computer modeling techniques. The personal computer provides negotiators with the ability to plug a variable into any deal equation and quickly get an answer as to how the modification on one component would affect the other components of the deal. In addition, the availability of on-line data bases has increased the negotiator's ability to do research.

The application of this information during the negotiation can be powerful in two ways: (1) having better information requires you to take less risk, and (2) the demonstration of your command of the essential information can be impressive.

Expertise. Expertise differs from information or knowledge in that the expert has mastered the utilization of the information and is generally perceived as the individual most able to make good use of the data. An example of this distinction between information and expertise can be found in an analogy drawn from medicine. A patient may have reams of medical data including x-rays, tests, lab reports, and personal observations by both the nursing staff and the other medical staff members. However, when it comes time to make some judgments about what to do with all this information, an expert is needed to synthesize and determine a correct course of action. In this sense, the expert relies on information; however, information in and of itself may not be helpful or useful without the expert.

There are a number of ways to establish expertise; these range from a show of credentials such as degrees, licenses, or certifications in a particular area, to references from other individuals who know the work of the expert. You can establish yourself as an expert during a negotiation through the presentation and application of your knowledge to the issues at hand.

Once perceived as an expert, a negotiator will find that the other side defers to his or her expertise on certain issues, thus ensuring more control of the process and a potentially better outcome.

Reward/Punishment. A strong source of power is the often perceived ability of one party to either reward or punish behavior. On one hand, if I agree to a discount that you are requiring from me as a salesperson, the reward I perceive may be in the commission I envision receiving as a result of this sale. On the other hand, if I grant you the discount requested, my management may reduce my commission, cut my territory, or in some other way fail to consider me for promotion or other career recognition. Salespeople often perceive the power of the buyer as very high since they control the reward system by which the salesperson lives. Getting an order is perceived as a reward, not getting it is perceived as a punishment.

In sales negotiation, it is important to consider the reward and punishment system that affects the purchaser. The purchaser needs to acquire goods and services from someone. The smart salesperson will consider what is important to the purchaser in their world of reward and punishment. How will the deal be perceived by the purchaser's management? How will the purchaser himself feel about the particular arrangements they have made?

Looking only at our own potential rewards and punishments is shortsighted. The probability of someone negotiating with you when they see no way in which you can help them is very limited. Conversely, there is the possibility that someone may engage you in negotiation if they perceive that there may be some way, either directly or subtly, that you could be in a punishing role for them. Even if that punishment is only withdrawal of service.

Legitimate/Positional. Another source of power is legitimate or positional power. Unlike expertise, which cannot be given, legitimate or positional power is given or bestowed. It is given in organizations in the form of titles such as president or director. Simple, but classic, examples of legitimate power could be the parental directive given to children, or the boss's directive to a subordinate, the doctor's orders to a patient, clergy to parishioner, or general to soldier.

Legitimate power can produce significant effects in a negotiation even though it depends very little on any other sources of power, like expertise, information, reward, or punishment. Legitimate power lies at the very foundation of much of our organizational, social, and family structures. A coach, a school principal, or a board member is often perceived as having a great deal of legitimate power over groups or individuals who look to them for guidance.

Legitimate power is subject to transience. If a person loses a title, then the power associated with it is also lost. Also, power is determined by the exclusivity of rank. One may be impressed by a person with the title of "vice president" until discovering there are 500 of them in the organization.

Identification/Association Power. Often, a person is perceived to have power because of identification or association with individuals or organizations that are perceived as powerful. Think of an IRS agent. Without the association with the reward/punishment authority of the agency, that agent might be perceived in the same light as any other junior accountant. A person who sits on a board of directors, or holds positions in civic, charitable, and social organizations, is perceived as having influence and connections. These connections are sources of power.

Referent/Moral Power. Referent or moral perceptions on the part of negotiators tend to limit or control certain negotiation issues. For example, if you or your company is known for consistently refusing to discount prices, chances are the discounting issue will not come up in negotiation, or if it is refused, the other side will not be surprised or adamant. Negotiators who have earned a very positive referent or moral reputation must be very careful not to deviate from the expected course of action—except by very careful and deliberate choice—as this type of power can be quickly diminished by behavior which is perceived as inconsistent with the image that has been created. A boss who has earned a very good reputation for dealing fairly with employees in salary negotiations, and one time makes a decision in haste that is perceived as unfair, quickly tarnishes his or her otherwise fair and equitable reputation.

Context

The last driver that affects a negotiation's outcome concerns the context within which the negotiation takes place. Take for example the arms negotiations between the United States and the Soviet Union. There are many influences and pressures on those negotiations that are separate from the main issues. How will the results appear to each country's political constituency? Will weakness or strength be perceived? If we come to an agreement, how will it affect our defense contractors? Our employment picture? Our economy in general?

Out of context, it appears in retrospect that the Allies made serious mistakes following World War II in their negotiations with the Soviets over the future of Eastern Europe. However, within context, the countries involved were weary of war and wanted the soldiers home. The prospect of additional hostilities involving a revitalized Soviet army would have been hard to sell.

Skilled negotiators always look at the "bigger picture," to avoid winning the battle (short term) and losing the war (long term). What other factors could be influencing the negotiation? How will this deal affect future negotiations?

Often a good deal can be made on single-occurrence negotiations. Such examples include a house that must be sold as part of a divorce settlement, a business where the partners don't get along, a lease where it is more important to have the "right" tenant than the highest rent, a car when inventories are high, etc. While we all experience our share of these single-occurrence negotiations, in business we are more likely to be facing the same people over the table time and time again. The relationships, both good and bad, that you have established with that supplier, that labor negotiator, and that employee will strongly influence future outcomes as additional reasons for negotiation arise.

CONCLUSION

An intelligent approach to negotiation begins with what you already know, and enhances this knowledge with skills and perceptions that involve:

Potential outcomes,

Conflict resolution and problem-solving techniques,

The applications of time, information, power, and context

Notes

[1] Princeton University Press, 1944.

[2] W. Donahue, *An Empirical Framework for Examining Negotiating Processes and Outcomes.* Communication Monographs No. 45.

[3] *Understanding Human Communication*, third ed. (New York: Holt, Rinehart, Winston, 1988), p. 175.

[4] *Interpersonal Conflict Resolution* (Glenview, IL: Scott, Foresman, 1975), p. 23.

[5] Robert Coulson, *Labor Arbitration: What You Need to Know*, Revised third ed. (New York: American Arbitration Association, 1988), p. 48.

[6] The Pareto Principle states that in most aspects of life a critical few efforts "around 20 percent" produce the great bulk of results, "around 80 percent." This has become known as the 80/20 Rule.

CHAPTER 3

Negotiation Strategies

Consider this question:

> Is it okay to plan to "trap your opponent during the planning of negotiations? If "trap" means to lie, cheat, steal, prepare false data, and so forth, the answer is no. But if "trap" means to plan to use acceptable strategies and tactics during the negotiation, the answer is yes. It is all right to plan to trap your opponent, and all negotiation professionals accept that. . . . A negotiation planning job is not complete unless you have considered what tactics you will use to win, or lose (if that is the plan), each issue to be negotiated.[1]

In the perfect world, everyone would use the same approach and achieving wise and equitable agreements would be a relatively uncomplicated process. Unfortunately, we do not live in the perfect world. In fact, in our research we have seen examples of deceit, false data and outright lies. Many of the people with whom you will be negotiating will not share your problem-solving mindset. The above quote comes from a very informative book on negotiation planning, *The Pre-*

Negotiation Planning Book, by William F. Morrison, a professional negotiator. Morisson is a purchaser, and may represent the prevailing point of view of his colleagues in the purchasing world. Tactics have by no means left the scene. Therefore, it is necessary for the skilled negotiator to become familiar with the many standard strategies and tactics used with the more adversarial and positional approaches.

To prepare yourself to deal effectively with adversarial approaches, take an inventory of your assets and liabilities in any particular negotiation.

FOCUS ON YOUR STRENGTH

Most negotiators underestimate the amount of strength they possess in the negotiating process. This is natural because you are more aware of how directly dependent *you* are on the outcome of the negotiation to provide you with achievement, satisfaction and, in fact, a living, than how the outcome may affect the other negotiator.

This is particularly true in sales negotiations. The negotiator on the other side may see handling corporate travel, making a lease decision or service purchase as only part of what he or she does—perhaps even a small part. So, although it is true that a salesperson can always seek other prospects, it is often easier for the current prospect to decide on another vendor than for the salesperson to begin all over with a new prospect.

In actuality, you have more strength than you might perceive at first glance. You can enhance your strength in a negotiation by believing and feeling that you have strength. The following are some points to focus on to negotiate from a position of strength.

> Because you are so close to your negotiation issues, your products, services, and needs, you know all the problems and shortcomings of your side of the issue. Nevertheless, while you are negotiating, *you must project a belief that the deal you are offering is the best available.* You can assume that the other negotiator is not a fool, and doesn't expect to get a perfect deal—just the best deal available. While you must anticipate outcomes and alternatives, you cannot negotiate effectively if you are overly concerned about what may go wrong.

Rely on your *skills as a negotiator* and your *expertise as a problem solver* to carry you through the rough spots.

There is great power in having done *thorough preparation*; knowing where you are going and truly knowing the needs of the other party.

You have the *power of persistence*. You are in a good position if you can focus all your attention and effort on the negotiation, while the other side must spread their efforts over a wider spectrum of responsibilities.

You have only gotten this far because they are interested in negotiating with you. Why would they be talking to you if they didn't see some potential benefit to them? Remember, difficult though it may be, *if you don't like the deal, you can walk away*. Walking away limits the other negotiator's options for solving his problems.

EXERCISE PATIENCE AND CONTROL

While time is a factor in all of our lives, and it would be wonderful if we could move things along at a more rapid pace, time is as much of a problem for the other negotiator as it is for you in most negotiations. In positional bargaining, most concessions will take place around the deadline.

Always *project a feeling of wanting to move the negotiation forward*, but you are willing to negotiate for as long as it takes.

Watch for any indication and do research to *determine if the other side is reaching some sort of deadline*; a mandate from management to have the issue settled by the beginning of the next budget year, the approach of a busy business period requiring the use of the services you provide, or a rising tide of complaints from the people who use the service.

You can guess when someone is reaching a deadline if you suddenly sense that you have power which was previously absent in your negotiations—a deference, a friendliness, a modification in tone, and a seeming willingness to make concessions. These cues are often subtle. An experienced purchaser will rarely communicate information about deadlines (or anything else).

There are some positive strategies that can enhance your approach.

EXPLORING OPTIONS

Exploring all of the possible options and alternatives and closely examining ideas that appear to be in conflict will generally help both sides to arrive at a satisfying solution.

Exploring options helps *establish an atmosphere of trust and a creative problem-solving climate*, while minimizing defensiveness.

Parties can progress toward a reworking and reshaping of their individual proposals to meet each other's needs.

In problem solving, people collaborate rather than compromise. In a compromise, each side gives up something they really want, and often neither side gets their needs met.

Generate options by asking "what if?" and "if/then" questions. Temporarily remove or alter restrictions. This opens up the potential for counter proposals and productive bargaining can then begin.

TRADEOFFS

Trading off is the process of weighing, sorting, evaluating, and deciding which of all possible options will work most effectively for you and the other person.

Both parties must work against having one or the other walk away from the negotiation feeling as if he or she hasn't received enough of a trade off compared to what has been perceived as given up.

In a tradeoff scenario, nothing is permanently settled, and serious damage can be done to the ongoing relationship.

When considering a tradeoff, always measure it in two ways: How it affects the other variables in your equation, and what you are getting for it from the other party.

Understand value and, if possible, add value to each option you have. You may not value one issue very highly, whereas the other negotiator may see it as crucial. Consider carefully and don't be too quick to trade off something that you see as minor, inexpensive, or no big problem. Look for the "quid pro quo" early, rather than a series of "gives" on your part with no corresponding concessions.

The more options there are on the table with perceived value for both parties, the easier the process of trading off becomes.

PERSONALIZING

In general, as organizations grow larger they seem to become more remote from the individuals who have to deal with them. People resent being treated like numbers or objects to be handled, manipulated, or discarded. If you are negotiating for a large company, you may have many benefits to offer. However, these can become obscured if the people you are negotiating with feel like a commodity.

Present yourself as a unique and vulnerable human being.

To maximize your impact as a negotiator, you must personalize both yourself and the situation.

The other parties must see you as a real person, not merely a number in a sequence, who has feelings, problems and needs like anyone else.

Instead of negotiating as if you were "The Company," negotiate on behalf of yourself as a representative of your company.

Train yourself to occasionally say, "I don't know," "I don't understand," or "I need your help."

Asking the other negotiator for help or an explanation tends to reinforce the joint problem-solving climate.

BRIDGING

No matter how difficult or protracted a negotiation has been, the odds are that you will most probably be negotiating with these same people again. Relationship building must be an integral part of the negotiating process.

Bridging develops a sense of continuity. You need to give the impression right from the start that you are the type of person who is and will continue to be available as the need arises. Good "consultative" negotiators give the impression that they will be available to serve the client's needs even after the deal is made.

If you have not built an adequate bridge, you will virtually have to start over again when it is time to renew or modify contracts.

Bridges are built with promises of follow-up, and the fulfillment of those promises.

Bridges are built when you deliver what you say you can and don't promise what you can't deliver.

Bridges must be maintained as well. If you interact with a client only when you are trying to sell something, the bridge will fall into disrepair.

Be sensitive to the other negotiator's attempts to build a bridge. "Don't call me, I'll call you," will blow the bridge.

COMPROMISE

We have discussed compromise at several different points so far, and we have not cast the approach in a very positive light. Compromise is going to remain a very important means of resolving conflict despite its perceived drawbacks. It occupies a space in our consciousness that will not easily be replaced by other methodologies.

Compromise has long been the world standard for mediation and conflict resolution; it is woven into the fabric of most governments and world organizations. While a list of successes could be produced for decades of compromise (or attempts at compromise) at the United Nations, the failures are far more in evidence.

In the United States we are taught throughout school that the democratic process is built on compromise, and we come to accept it as the preferred mode of settling disputes. In many instances, compromise does provide the best possible alternative. Not all conflicts lend themselves to a collaborative or problem-solving approach. The error in negotiation is the predilection toward seeking compromise in those situations where collaboration would better serve both parties.

Collaborative or problem-centered negotiation begins with a problem-solving mindset. It requires that at least one and preferably both of the bargainers are willing to admit that there may be alternatives not yet perceived that will resolve the conflict to everyone's advantage.

Suffice it to say that the more you know about communication in general, the better your chances to succeed at negotiation. Among the constructs that influence negotiation outcomes are some which the negotiators bring with them psychologically, and are not part of the substance of the negotiation, yet have an important effect on the relationship. Style of negotiating is one such element, and will be discussed in detail in Chapter 5.

Another construct that can have an important effect on the outcome is the matter of who controls the "rules" by which the communication takes place.

CONTROLLERS VERSUS UNDERSTANDERS

The rules governing communication in a negotiation are largely created interpersonally by the participants themselves. Research in interpersonal communication indicates that in the process of creating a rule system, people bring with them differing motives and objectives. Nowhere is this more true than in negotiation.

The rules are also dictated situationally by the externally imposed relationship of the negotiating parties, such as buyer and seller, boss and subordinate, husband and wife, parent and child. There are two fundamental orientations toward interpersonal rule structure in communication: an orientation toward *understanding* the behaviors of others and an orientation toward *controlling* the behaviors of others.[2] These orientations grow out of the individual needs of each party.

Basically, a need reflects a psychological state, in which some input from a person's environment necessary to his or her perceived well-being is either lacking or potentially lacking. To fulfill this need, a person develops strategies designed to achieve certain ends; in most cases, the temporary satisfaction of needs.

An individual's values determine the constraints placed on the strategies. They dictate which strategies are permissible and which are not. Unfortunately for the buyer or seller, boss or subordinate, the other person's experiences can create values that do not limit what strategies are acceptable professionally or ethically.

Controllers manifest a basic need to assume command over other people. Because of what may be a deeply held sense of vulnerability or desire for power, they focus on achieving power positions in all relationships. Controllers develop a set of intentions in keeping with their needs; they formulate and execute communication strategies designed to put them in dominant positions. They tend to be continually in conflict with others since they see others as threats to their security or position, and are more comfortable giving orders than developing communication relationships.

Understanders, however, have a basic need to figure out what they themselves, as well as other people, are like and what they need. They enjoy developing close personal relationships and prefer to keep conflict at a minimum.[3] The collaborative, problem-solving approaches suggested in this book develop message strategies that maximize the probability of opening relationships. When compared with controllers in this light, understanders employ a different value system, putting the freedom of others roughly on a par with their own.

Most controllers and most understanders possess a mixture of both sets of needs, and values; and neither operates on the basis of one set or the other all of the time. Even so, the type of orientation preferred exerts an influence on the interpersonal rule system that emerges. Chapter 5 will discuss how these needs interact with each other and various other factors to create distinct negotiating styles.

When a controller and an understander interact in a negotiation, the controller often attempts to force his or her game plan on the understander. In certain situations where roles are situationally determined, such as boss-subordinate or company president and salesperson (vendor), the senior person is in a position to dictate the rule-setting process. The other party needs to use understanding as part of the negotiating strategy, and to work toward gaining some control of the process. The understander adapts his or her communication to the controller's game plan. This accommodation does not mean that the understander will allow the controller to completely take over; but it means the understander has the capacity and perspective to assess whose needs seem more important at a particular time. The understander generally permits the controller to define the rule system.

In defining the rule system, the controller demands that his or her brand of structural and content rules govern the communication situation: "Either we do it my way, or we won't do it at all." The RFP (Request For Proposal) is the classic example— rigid rules, detached, and little if any relationship. Controllers react to conflict by attempting to unilaterally define the situation so that it is satisfactory for them, without regard for the other. Understanders deal with conflict by trying to define the situation in mutually satisfying ways.

As a negotiator sitting across the table from a particularly tough positional bargainer whose position or importance in the context of the negotiation is superior to yours, you probably have little choice in the role you play—you are the understander. What can you do to offset and resolve the difficulties of this kind of rule structure in a negotiation? Begin with as thorough an understanding of what (and whom) you are dealing with as soon as possible. Assess your own feelings. Do you feel as though your needs are not being considered and will not be satisfied? Are you tempted to lower your aspiration levels? There are no easy and fast solutions to this problem; however, there are some strategies you can use to help work your way through the situation.

De-Labeling

The person you are dealing with may have some very definite stereotyped labels for you. "Salesman" has a whole range of negative associations in the minds of some buyers. Likewise, a salesperson may harbor negative stereotypes of the buyer. The strategy begins with your own perception of how you have been labeled. What is the other person's attitude telling you? Look for nonverbal clues to tip you off as to how the person you are dealing with has labeled you.

Find ways to act or respond that are inconsistent with how you have been negatively labeled. The other negotiator will attempt to find ways to force you to respond according to the label. The longer you maintain behavior that is contradictory to what is expected, the better your chances of breaking through.

Monitor your own tendency to label others. Anyone who has spent some time outside of the negotiation situation with a controller may discover a decent hard-working family oriented person who can crack a joke once in a while and even gives to charity. The key is to try to see that person as the one who is negotiating, and respond to the person and not the mask.

Controlling the Pace

If the situation is such that you cannot control the rules of communication—at least initially—then seek to control the pace of communication.

It is important in any case not to allow yourself to be rushed into agreement. Positional negotiators like single-issue bargaining, that is to take items one at a time and to close the issue on each in turn.

You have to continually assert that all issues are open until they are all agreed on because they are interrelated and any change in one will affect the others.

When presented with an apparently over-controlling, inflexible positional bargaining approach, you can respond by calling a recess to consider their position, generate new options, and consult with others in your own organization.

Using Humor

While controllers use black-and-white thinking, they don't necessarily set out to make you lose—they just want to win. You can't permit the other negotiator to maintain the rule-setting position throughout, or you will most probably wind up with a bad deal if you can deal at all. One strategy involves the use of humor. When someone presents you with a list of demands and insists that responses be provided promptly and in order, making light of it can go a long way toward reducing the conflict. Restate both sides in a humorous light. Be careful that your manner or tone is not a condescending one. This accomplishes two things:

1. It reduces the tension of the situation,
2. It shows the other person that his or her side has been considered.

For example:

Prospect	Listen, I'm not going to fool around with you people. I want a bigger discount, no liability, and customized reports or we have very little to talk about.
Salesperson	Is that all? Just a bigger discount, no liability, and customized reports? Why are you being so easy on us?

Don't Be a Victim

Perhaps the hardest, and yet the most important thing to remember during a negotiation is that regardless of what you are getting back across the table, you are close to closing a deal. Granted that being close is not the same as closing one, but the person negotiating with you is not doing it for the sheer fun of it. You have gotten this far because there is interest—at some level—in doing business with you. The person across the table is under some measure of pressure to conclude an agreement successfully, or explain why he or she did not.

Remember, as hard as it may appear to be, you must be prepared to walk away from a deal that is not good for you. Don't get into negotiations until you have given yourself options so you can walk away. Chances are that if you have done your homework, you know the levels at which the deal will be profitable. If you can't make money on the deal, the competition probably can't either.

Controllers are often rewarded for their behavior through the achievement of limited objectives. One criticism that is often leveled at controllers is that they miss the bigger picture while focusing on minute details or winning their way. However, it is not a matter of missing the bigger picture; the controller's life is a constant communication trial. He or she is forced to spend so much time embroiled in rule-centered conflicts and searching for additional means of control that it becomes impossible to experience the satisfaction of a problem-solving negotiation.

CONCLUSION

Understanding the rules and structure of negotiation provides the basis for your objectivity and emotional control. Many people enter a negotiation as if the communication dynamics are a free-form happening that can go in any direction. In fact, many people find this uncertainty (winging it) exciting and energizing. However, more often than not, this approach is a formula for ending up on the short end of a deal managed by someone who really did his homework.

Skilled negotiators focus as much on the dynamics of the communication as they do on the components of the deal. They want to know as much as possible about the other negotiator—temperament, style, and experience.

Thus being prepared for negotiation means more than knowing what you need for a good deal. It means knowing yourself as a psychological being, and sensitizing yourself to the psychological cues of others. Somewhere between the emotional needs of the parties and

the limitations of the context is a space where effective communication becomes possible, and with it, the potential for collaboration—
an appropriate balance of control and understanding. The interaction
of these behavioral components and the negotiation situation are de-
terminants of negotiation style (Chapter 5) and they influence the
tactics (Chapter 4) used in a particular negotiation.

Notes

[1] William F. Morrison, *The Pre-Negotiation Planning Book* (New York: Wiley,
1985), p. 95. Reprinted by permission of John Wiley & Sons, Inc. Copyright © 1985,
John Wiley & Sons, Inc.

[2] Mark Steinberg and Gerald R. Miller, "Interpersonal Communication: A Sharing
Process" in Gerhard J. Hanneman and William McEwen, *Communication and Behavior*
(Reading, MA: Addison-Wesley, 1975), p. 133.

[3] Steinberg and Miller "Interpersonal Communication," p. 134.

CHAPTER 4

Negotiation Tactics

No book on negotiation is complete without a discussion of some of the identifiable tactics that frequently arise during the negotiation process. We have already made our case for the view that we are currently in a transitional phase in approaches to negotiation. That is, we are moving away from the win-lose adversarial and lose-lose compromise approaches toward the no-lose collaborative approach. We are experiencing more problem-centered negotiation styles on both a national and a personal level.

However, anyone who negotiates must be wary of the uninitiated or unconvinced bargainer who has achieved a large measure of success through hard positional bargaining laced with tactics, driven by blind competitiveness, and to whom the crossing of moral and ethical boundaries to win may not seem inappropriate. After all, in hard positional bargaining, the view that "all's fair in love and war and negotiating" is something you need to be prepared for.

When you are confronted with such a bargainer, do not abandon your collaborative approach; at the same time, you need to be aware of what certain tactics are intended to accomplish so that you can respond effectively. It is in this context that we offer the following discussion of tactics. We do not advocate that you employ them in your bargaining. You are urged to prepare an adequate defense when they appear.

The following nine tactics represent the most prominent tactics still in frequent use in business negotiations. There are others that come into play in diplomacy and labor relations that are not in keeping with the deal-making focus of this book.

EXTREME DEMANDS

Taking an extreme position has been called different names by different theorists. You may have encountered it in other texts as a "demand avalanche" or "Soviet style." The element of the extreme is what identifies this tactic. It is a situation where at the outset the other negotiator makes very high demands:

"We need a 5 percent rebate on our travel."

"To me, this company is worth one half the asking price."

"In addition to a lower price per square foot, we expect full maintenance, partitions, new phone cables, an upgrade on the air conditioning, painting once each year, carpeting in the executive offices, and, oh yes, paper for the johns."

The extreme opening position is an attempt to force you to lower your expectations. Whenever we are confronted with a large demand or a list of demands, even when we have no intention of giving in, there is a natural tendency to consider what is feasible. The sheer weight of an extreme demand or of several demands in a series, pushes us toward making concessions.

It would be easy to say, "Don't make concessions" as a way of counteracting this tactic. However, there are some specific behaviors that you can affect that will help you promote and maintain a problem-centered approach even when confronted with extreme demands.

Research has shown that successful negotiators maintain a strong position by using a variety of arguments, by making more offers, by frequently changing the topic and rejecting the offers of others. This pattern of action and reaction balances extreme demands and threats with supporting comments and concessions.

These results were derived from studying negotiation in the collective bargaining environment, so some differences from typical business situations may be expected. However, the successful negotiators in this study seemed to understand how to avoid "conflict spirals." A conflict spiral develops when there is an escalation of attacking and defending between the negotiators without corresponding regression in the form of support and concession. The result is usually stalemate.

Further research indicated that one sure way to create a conflict spiral is by reciprocating the other side's tactics. These points will be useful to keep in mind for the handling of many of the tactics discussed in this chapter.

The following suggestions may provide you with some direction when dealing with extreme demands.

Restate the demand in terms that are more acceptable to you: "So, what you are saying, Mr. Jones, is that you would like to discuss the packaging of several items into the total deal for the lease."

Reinforce your expectation level. State your objective as reaching a fair and reasonable agreement that satisfies the interests of both parties; that such an agreement is necessary "if we are going to do business together." This alludes to your ability and willingness to walk away.

Do not reciprocate with your own list. Often if you avoid stating a position at the outset, you can move the general approach of the other side closer to the problem-solving methodology we have been discussing.

Responses to Avoid

We have observed the extreme demand tactic applied with frequency and effectiveness in several financial services negotiations. The factors that typically elicit this tactic are the multicomponent characteristics of the deal and the relative power positions of the negotiators involved—a salesperson on one side and a purchaser in the role of chief financial officer, investment manager, administrative officer, and so forth, on the other side.

Often the buyer of services has researched what other buyers have gotten and accordingly prepares a wish list of components that should

be included in the deal. We have also observed a tendency in salespeople to conduct their sales calls in laundry list fashion; that is,
providing the purchaser at the outset with a complete list of components that are available without regard for the actual need or value of
these components to the client.

When you are subjected to the extreme demands tactic, you should
watch for the other negotiator to back off a little on a few points. The
temptation when this happens will be for you to concede the remaining points because the deal now looks much better than it did before.
The psychological relief felt when the other side backs off can cause
you to overlook the fact that you have conceded more than you
initially intended. Concession reinforces the use of this tactic, and it
will come at you again.

PLAY ACTING

Some negotiators use emotional responses such as getting angry,
raising their voice, or indicating that they think you are trying to take
advantage of them. The key effect of this strategy is the surprise it
creates. Also, depending on your particular psychological make-up,
the tactic may instill feelings of guilt causing you to desire to make
amends. Sometimes negative comments are made about you or your
company. Language is intensified to make you lower your expectations, to put you on the defensive and to cause you to make concessions to prove that you aren't as bad as they seem to think you are.

The use of intense language as a persuasive device has been the
subject of some study, and the results are interesting from a negotiation standpoint. If the negotiators have equal power, such as a lessor
with several potential renters and a lessee with several potential sites,
high intensity messages delivered by one or the other will not be more
persuasive.

If one person takes a position that is at odds with the other, the
receiver psychologically refutes the arguments as they are heard. This
creates a "backlash" that can actually work against influencing a
change in attitude or position. Between negotiators of equal power
and equal ego involvement in the importance of the issue, the research shows that low-intensity, or less dramatic messages produce the
greatest attitude shift.

However, if the relative power positions are unequal, as they often are in sales negotiation or any other circumstance where one party has more options than the other, the intensity of the language and the argument can have a very persuasive effect. Language intensity comes at you from two sources, the use of qualifiers and the use of metaphor. Qualifiers indicate certainty or extremity.

"We are going to make a deal by the end of this week whether it involves you or not." (Certainty)

"I despise the way this contract has been drawn." (Extremity)

Metaphors compare the current situation with something highly charged with emotion. The most frequent metaphors allude to either sex or death.

"Listen, you guys aren't going to rape us on this deal if I have anything to say about it."

"If you won't assume the liability for environmental hazards, you're going to kill this deal."

"That will happen over my dead body."

Depending on the quality of the play acting, it may be difficult to determine if you are being subjected to a tactic or if the other party is genuinely upset over something. In either case, the following are some suggestions for dealing with this situation.

Don't be thrown off guard and begin to experience guilt feelings.

The best response to an emotional strategy is either (1) no response and a pause to allow them to continue when you don't respond as expected, or (2) wait for the moment to pass, then restate or paraphrase the last point you made, and ask the other negotiator to clarify or expand on his or her concern.

Ask if there are additional objections or concerns not yet uncovered that could account for such strong feeling.

If the emotion won't abate, request a recess until a later time when things can be discussed calmly.

A more risky approach to be taken only when others fail is to state openly that you perceive the emotion is merely a tactic and it will not work.

Responses to Avoid

Play acting can occur in any type of negotiation, since it is a "context" tactic rather than a "content" tactic. Often, negotiators are drawn into the theatrics of the moment and respond with some play acting of their own. The reasoning might be, "This will show them that I am not a pushover. If they want yelling, I'll give them yelling!" This is almost a sure way to produce a conflict spiral leading to a stalemate. Yes, we've all heard those stories about the guy who yelled back and ended up earning the respect of the opposition, but, proceed with caution.

The pitfall is to allow yourself to be intimidated by the tactic, and to begin making concessions as a way to appease the seemingly emotional other party. Either way, by either responding in kind or conceding points to the other side, you are allowing the other negotiator to control your responses. You will lose track of your plan and reinforce the use of this strategy against you.

LIMITED AUTHORITY

"Look, this is the best I can do. You have to drop the liability requirement. My management feels it's not their problem. If I have to open it up with them again, it could take forever. Two of them are out of town until. . . ."
"What can I tell you. It's not up to me. The decision was made upstairs that we must have the 7 percent reduction, and a two-week commitment on turnaround."

When the limited authority tactic was used, the other side will often offer you a settlement option; "if you want to close this deal right now, we can do it based on the items I have enumerated. However, I don't have the authority to change these points, and the issue will have to be taken to my superiors." The tactic is designed to put stress on you to accept less-than-favorable conditions rather than have to go through the entire process again and risk losing the deal altogether. The objective is to get you to accept the proposal as presented, or to make a counterproposal that is more favorable for the other side than you intended.

It has been paradoxical in our observations that negotiators who use limited authority most often actually do have the power to move the deal forward, but blame others for making demands that they are actually initiating. Whereas, people who have truly limited authority, generally act just the opposite. They don't want you to know that their power is limited. This is not always the case, but it is worth considering when you are presented with the limited authority tactic.

Some suggestions for dealing with this tactic are:

The best defense against the limited authority strategy is to qualify the other negotiator first. Is he or she the decision maker? This is best addressed early in the negotiation before defensiveness or sensitivity become major issues.

Asking, "How have decisions of this type been handled in the past?" can give general procedural insights, and alert you to contradictions in your negotiation relative to previous deals.

If you are surprised by the limited authority tactic, suggest that you have the same problem and perhaps a meeting could be arranged between your decision makers and their decision makers to most directly resolve the issue.

If it is a ploy, the other side will often "find" his or her lost authority. If it is true, you may be able to gain a commitment to an important next step. Be careful not to raise defensiveness or to embarrass the other party. Sincere, problem-centered interest can be very effective.

In any case, do not allow yourself to be rushed into an agreement.

Responses to Avoid

The tendency will be for you to want to immediately propose another solution that you do not want but is less costly than the one you have been offered. As good as such an alternative may appear on the spur of the moment, chances are it is not as good as you think it is. You haven't had time to work it through. Also, you may miss the opportunity to reopen other issues that would balance the deal, and to test the reality of the limited authority you are facing. Failing to test may also signal your vulnerability to other tactics.

If you give in to the demand because you are afraid of the risk of losing the deal, you demonstrate weakness, a susceptibility to time pressure, and you have reinforced the use of this strategy in negotiating with you.

TAKE IT OR LEAVE IT

This strategy is often couched in terms that suggest that the other negotiator has already achieved the objectives desired through negotiation with one or more of your competitors, or some other party who is seemingly in a position to satisfy the substance of the need being negotiated.

> "Well, I have to tell you that your competition is offering me the same material at the same price and they are picking up the delivery charges."
>
> "I have a proposal from ABC Realty for the same square footage in a comparable building for $17.00 a foot. Now, I'd like to do business with you, but $18.50 is out of line."

Another application of this tactic, which is used particularly early on in the negotiation process, forces you toward one issue and away from the other components of the deal.

"I know for a fact that you are offering XYZ Company a 5 percent discount." Take it or leave it is an attempt to undercut your feelings of power in a negotiation and to lower your expectation level. If you can't match the deal, the other negotiator wants you to raise the ante as close to the other deal as possible. Also, by forcing you to deal with one issue at a time (single-issue bargaining), the deal gets tilted in the other party's favor.

As a typical power strategy, take it or leave it requires one negotiator to emphasize the difference between himself or herself and the other party in terms of regard and control. The approach assumes that those with lesser power, of whatever type, will usually comply with the wishes advocated by the greater power. Most discussions of power strategies consider specific techniques such as laws and judicial decisions (legitimate political power), job advancement or other financial well-being (reward/punishment economic power), and the doctrines of fundamentalist religions, corporate culture, or business philosophies (moral/referent power). While all of these play a part in negotiation, another often overlooked is physical power. To put it another way, power strategies are enhanced if used by a negotiator with strong physical presence. One organization with which we are familiar, and in fact have negotiated with for assignments over the years, has a cultural tendency to hire very large men. The typical negotiation scenario begins with lunch at a particular club where there is a scale in the lobby. Everyone actually weighs in before sitting at the table!

However, many theorists tell us that actually possessing some amount of power may be insufficient. It does no good to threaten someone with control over their political, economic, moral or physical rewards, if the person being threatened does not feel you are capable of carrying out the threat or if that person simply decides to pay the consequences out of sheer obstinacy (another type of conflict spiral). This is how we end up with huge skyscrapers built around small single-family homes that wouldn't sell out.

Those who tend to use power strategies are sensitive to this fact, and, although they come on strong, they are reluctant to push too hard if they see the tactic is not working. With this as a backdrop, we offer the following suggestions for dealing with this tactic.

In order to counteract this tactic, you must have a complete understanding of the cost side of your deal and be responsive to the guidelines set in your planning process.

If you are presented with a deal that you know cannot work for you, chances are good that it cannot work for any of your competitors either.

Respond by resummarizing the benefits your deal can provide, noting that in order to provide a favorable (profitable) outcome for both parties, the deal at the level the other party is suggesting would be unprofitable and unacceptable.

After "hanging tough" for awhile, if you have something left to give, offer it as a face-saving gesture for the other negotiator.

To be effective against this strategy, however, you must be willing to walk away from a deal that is clearly unprofitable.

Responses to Avoid

You may have the tendency to avoid the conflict created by this tactic, and, as such, walk away from a deal that could have been consummated with a little perseverance.

Another danger is agreeing to resolve the conflict issue by issue, thereby losing sight of the balance of issues that constitute the entire deal. Another variant of this response is to compare the other "offer" with your deal on a point-by-point basis. This potentially highlights some deficiencies in your offer that will then become important bargaining points for the other side.

GOOD GUY/BAD GUY

A senior person you haven't met before attends a session where you are presenting some proposals based on the needs as you have identified them. After listening to most of your presentation, he interrupts, stands up and says: "Why are you guys wasting my time with this? What I've heard is totally out of scale with my thinking and it's not going to fly. And, (addressing his subordinate) George, I want to talk to you this afternoon." He stalks out of the room.

A person introduced as a member of the committee then says: "Listen, we used your system at my last company, and, frankly, I think we got a raw deal!"

It is not unusual for a negotiator to be confronted with a "bad guy" second party at some point in the negotiation—generally at a higher level or at least parallel to the decision maker—who appears to have some authority over the outcome. This bad guy makes extreme and unreasonable demands and does it very convincingly, leaving you with the feeling that unless significant concessions are made, there will be no deal. At a later point in the negotiation, the original decision maker, or "good guy", presents a more moderate position that seems reasonable by comparison.

The objective of this tactic is to force you into making several quick concessions in order to provide ammunition for the good guy to reopen the negotiation with the unreasonable party. The tactic also serves to put you on the defensive and causes the control and momentum to shift to the other side.

Anyone who has ever seen a police show on television understands instinctively how good guy/bad guy works. In spite of that, it remains one of the most frequently used and successful tactics in practice today. What follows are some suggestions for dealing with this tactic.

This is another tactic designed to lower your aspiration level. The best defense is to regroup your thoughts around your prenegotiation plan.

You can even suggest a recess to consider the new demands, but on your return offer no concessions.

In some instances it may be advisable to bring in your own bad guy.

Once a bad guy enters the picture, assume that everyone you're dealing with—no matter how seemingly benign—is a bad guy.

Responses to Avoid

There is a danger that you may accept the ploy at face value and walk away from a deal that would have eventually worked out for both parties. In a sales negotiation, you may provide an opportunity for a competitor by not continuing to pursue your prospect energetically.

The other possibility is that you will fall into the trap and make serious concessions to appease the bad guy. Doing this encourages continued use of this tactic, and will ultimately result in a deal that is not balanced in your favor.

PHONY ISSUES

"I think if we can work through our differences on the price, we may be able to handle the other matters quickly. So, let's settle that now."

"The key issue for me is rebate. I've got to have one to make this deal work. Now, what can you do for us?"

Phony issue bargaining (or feinting) occurs when the other negotiator seems to place inordinate emphasis on one issue in the negotiation, for example, management reports or service levels, to divert attention from the real objective—a rebate or a lower price. The purpose is to get you to offer concessions on the real but under-emphasized objective in order to placate the demands surrounding the phony objective.

In another form of phony issue bargaining the negotiator will present false information about a supposed deal already cut and ready to be signed with another party that is substantially more favorable than the one you are offering. This sets both a false goal and a false deadline, both of which put great pressure on you to make concessions.

The objective of this tactic is to get your attention focused on one issue to divert attention from another issue that holds more importance to the other side. You may offer what the other negotiator wants simply to help yourself out on the phony issue. Even if the item being sought is of low value to you, it could be of high value to the other side. Giving it away easily, limits your ability to bargain on additional issues. When the other side focuses on price, the real issue may be service guarantees. When the focus is on financing, the real issue may be the closing date.

The following are some ideas for dealing with this tactic.

The best defense against phony issues is careful listening, and clarifying what is really important to the other side. You are in the best position to know if what you are hearing could actually be true.

No one, not even your competitors, is interested in cutting a deal that loses money. Here, again, you must know the cost side of your deal and that of your competition.

Stick to your guidelines and your prenegotiation plan. Without being confrontational, allow a note of skepticism to creep into your responses by using more mirroring behavior to identify real needs and discrepancies in the deal.

Response to Avoid

If you are not careful, you may allow yourself to be drawn into single-issue bargaining and begin offering concessions on secondary issues to appease the other negotiator on the issue that is being over-emphasized. In the worst case, you may end up giving away things that are both important and unimportant to the other side, but could have been used as bargaining chips to cut a better deal for yourself.

Another problematic option is to call the other party's bluff on a supposed deal, or accuse the other side of not bargaining in good faith. This response can put you into a conflict spiral, and may cause the other negotiator to seek another deal in order to save face. Rarely can someone be embarrassed into a deal.

JUST ONE MORE THING

"We liked your proposal adjustments very much, and we have decided to go with the deal. I want to compliment you on the way you have handled these negotiations. I made one note on the proposal that gives us a bit more stretch on the payment terms."

"We met on your final proposal yesterday. We got lucky because it's the last time for awhile that the entire committee will be in town. Everything slipped through like a breeze—except we needed to add another half of a percent on the interest."

This tactic occurs in many forms, but two common applications involve the "decision is made" or fait accompli approach at the beginning of a negotiation and the last minute add-on at the end of the negotiation. In discussing this tactic with negotiators, we are amazed at how often they say they are presented with a deal that supposedly has already received the approval of management and would be difficult or impossible to change.

This tactic is often combined with a phony issue in which the negotiator may also state that at least one of your competitors has already agreed to take this deal. At other times, your proposal or even a submitted contract will be returned to you signed, but with one or more items crossed out or altered. The effect here is to pressure you to accept the alteration instead of reopening the negotiation. The objective of this tactic is to put pressure on you to accept the demand in order to close the deal now, rather than risking delay or losing the deal altogether.

The reason this tactic is so effective can be explained by the principles outlined in balance theory. A psychologist, named Fritz Heider[1] postulated that unbalanced states produce tension and generate forces to restore balance. This imbalance, as when a contract you thought you had wrapped up shows up with amendments, creates a climate that is susceptible to change. Or, to put it another way, you may be willing to change your position to restore the balance of having closed a deal.

The defenses against this tactic involve maintaining your perspective of the total negotiation process. Some suggestions for doing this are:

> When presented with a fait accompli, you must perceive it as part of the negotiation process rather than as a substitute for negotiation.

> Recognize that the deal agreed to represented a balanced positioning of many components. You may need to reconsider all the components related to the new request.

> "The show isn't over until the fat lady sings," is a favorite phrase among skilled negotiators. Treat any fait accompli you are presented with as a counter proposal and respond accordingly, that is, as if you were in an earlier stage of the negotiation.

> A signed contract is meaningless if the deal doesn't satisfy your interests; therefore, the negotiation must continue.

Responses to Avoid

You may agree with the demand without thinking, or give in to the need to restore balance. The result could drop the profit margin on the deal to zero. When you make a concession on a single issue, you lose an opportunity to balance the effect on the other components of the deal.

In another situation you reject the request out of frustration, without exploring the need and seeking a viable solution. This could produce a stalemate, cause a time gap, and provide an opportunity for someone else to propose a deal that is equally, or more, acceptable than yours.

SLICING

> At the first meeting: "On that interest rate, can we lock it in at another quarter of a percent?"

> Next meeting: "I think we can sell the deal upstairs if I can tell them I'm getting one extra report run for headquarters."

Third meeting: "Can you do anything for us on customizing the MIS reports?"

Fourth meeting: "If I agree to this entire package, I'll need an extra half of a percent guarantee on the renewal."

This strategy (sometimes called scaling down or "salami") involves taking each separate component of a deal and negotiating it at the best possible level. The other negotiator wants to give the impression that he or she doesn't really need many of the features you are offering, but may buy a few of them if the price is right. Once the other negotiator feels he or she has gone as far as possible on the items individually, you will be asked to make additional concessions if the entire package is bought.

Using a series of small requests detracts from how they will add up to a total package. The objective of this tactic is to give you the feeling that it is not worth risking the entire deal over seemingly small issues. In addition, you are positioned so that you have more difficulty balancing the relative values of the total deal. This tactic will continue until the very end when you will be asked to make one additional concession to close the deal.

Slicing is a very common tactic in a buyer/seller negotiation. Purchasing people use it with great frequency and with great effect. Some things to keep in mind when dealing with this tactic include:

The best defense is awareness. Keep all of the components of the package in front of you.

At each juncture, evaluate how a shift in conditions surrounding one variable will affect other variables in the equation.

When you are offered a settlement on one issue, question it to understand and prioritize its importance relative to the overall deal. Use the if/then approach. "If I agree to the higher price, then will you take on the environmental liability?"

Know what concessions you want. Establish a quid pro quo format early, without becoming trite. The other side must have the sense that any request they make of you will cost them something in return. This may shape their requests more realistically.

Discuss all components and make the necessary adjustments to the deal's range and issues as you go along without committing to agreement on each issue. This way you circumvent the package deal ploy at the end.

Responses to Avoid

If you give in to each request as it occurs because you feel you can't let the deal fall through for such a little amount, you are responding in serial form and will lose track of the total package. You will be surprised at what it all adds up to.

If you become aware of the tactic and become progressively less flexible about concessions, you will be moving toward a potential deadlock. Your frustration will cause you to forget that previous concessions can now be traded off or you can require that reciprocal concessions be made.

In another scenario, you make a pact with yourself that you'll block the next request, regardless. In so doing, you blind yourself to the fact that the next request, might have been beneficial to both parties.

THE SECRET AGENT

"I want you to understand, we didn't call you in here to discuss what goes on in our business, we want to know what you can do for us. Our people feel they can do just as well with costs in-house as you can on the outside."

"We're not even convinced we need to use your services. You tell us what you think the advantages would be, and we'll see if it makes sense."

Some negotiators, particularly those with the purchasing agent mindset, are convinced they will get a better deal if they are in control of more information than you are. It is a common strategy to conceal their true interests, needs, and priorities. This approach grows out of a general mistrust of salespeople. The effect is to make the salesperson offer more when the purchaser might have been willing to accept less. It also causes the salesperson to fall back on laundry list selling rather than using the client-centered or need-satisfaction approach.

This approach blocks you from uncovering the other party's real needs. It interferes with the problem-solving approach to negotiating and puts control of the communication rules in the hands of the other negotiator. The objective is to cause you to lay out additional available features and options that you might not have had any intention of doing in order to close a deal.

This is an extremely difficult tactic to counteract. The following are some suggestions for working your way through it.

Rapport-building behavior is very important here State the benefits of being collaborative and working together.

You must find out as much as possible about the person you are dealing with; this includes his or her position in the company, how previous negotiations with your company or others have been handled and, personal and family relationships. All these elements become potential avenues for reaching the person behind the secret agent tactic.

Spend more time on chitchat (e.g., children, sports, current events). Seek out some common ground in order to build trust. Demonstrate your ability and willingness as a listener rather than as a talker. The use of questions to show interest in the concerns of the other side can accelerate the building of trust.

Emphasize the problem-solving aspect of your discussion. You may need to assert that your style requires more thoroughness, and you can't work in the dark if you are going to put together a good deal.

Do not abandon your problem-solving approach in the interests of moving the negotiation along more quickly.

Responses to Avoid

If you are susceptible to being put on the defensive, you may begin laying out the components of a deal before understanding what the other person's needs are. You could be offering more than the other negotiator expected.

Alternatively, you should not lock horns and say, "We can't give you an answer until we know more about what you want." This creates a conflict spiral leading to a stalemate. If the other side has a bias toward secrecy based on a general mistrust of people seeking to persuade, you will be playing into that bias. "These guys are always trying to get into your head so they can put one over on you."

CONCLUSION

We began this chapter with the notion that in the perfect world everyone would approach the resolution of conflict with the same problem-solving mindset. We do not live in the perfect world. Most of us find it necessary to use negotiation as part of our business, and our personal and professional lives. We come by our understanding of negotiation through trial and error and the observation of others. We encounter negotiators who employ tactics maybe not as a conscious move to take advantage of others, but because that's the way they have learned to negotiate. When we are confronted with any of the tactics we have discussed in this chapter, it is important to remember that this is not a signal to abandon our problem-solving approach, but rather an indication to be on guard and redouble our efforts to break through to an agreement which is mutually beneficial.

The most effective overall approach to handling tactics is not to give in and allow the other side to benefit at your expense. As Socrates said, "Know thyself." Nowhere is this more true than when you are sitting at the negotiating table. Regardless of the approach the other negotiator may take, remember that he or she needs an agreement as badly as you do; what differs is how such an agreement is sought by each side. The value of any deal is measured by the relative satisfaction of the negotiators in terms of dollars, effort, psychological rewards, and the condition of the relationships left behind. Will you be able to turn every negotiating effort into a model for problem-solving, no-lose agreements? Of course not. Learn to measure your success in incremental terms rather than absolutes. The more you are able to avoid employing or succumbing to tactics in your negotiating, the more effective you will be as a negotiator—and as a person.

Notes

[1] *The Psychology of Interpersonal Relations* (New York: Wiley, 1958).

CHAPTER 5

The Role of Style in Negotiating

The president and CEO of a major service company spoke to us about his varied career, which had placed him in many interesting negotiation situations. He shared with us some of his negotiating experiences from his days with a major chemical company and from more recent examples of negotiating service contracts.

The following is an excerpt of the interview we conducted with him.

President: I worked for one of the most wonderful bosses at the beginning of my career, and he was a mentor for all the divisional presidents at the chemical firm. He provided me with a great deal of freedom and challenge as part of my development. For a person of my age and experience, I had some unusual opportunities. I was given the task to negotiate a contract with a multibillion dollar customer, who was having some quality problems with one of his processes and wanted us to supply a component for an intermediate step in a batch process.

We predetermined that we could provide the material they needed for three cents a pound. They had indicated that they just needed it for new business. However, I learned that they were having serious quality problems. I told them we couldn't do it for less than eight cents—figuring that they were only going to use us as long as necessary and cast us aside at the end. I also wanted to leave some room for negotiation. I saw no reason at all to be anything other than optimistic. You can sense when somebody is between a rock and a hard place. They took the deal at the price stated with minimal resistance.

The really ironic thing is that years later, I had the opportunity to openly—and without risk—talk to the person that I negotiated with. He had moved to another employer. I had the opportunity to ask the question, "How much would you have paid?" He gave me the feeling that they would have paid anything within reason because they had a multimillion dollar installation coming down around their ears. Up until then I had felt great about the victory of eight cents; then he told me we could have charged more. By not asking for twenty cents a pound though, we stopped them from going out and looking at other sources. At eight cents, they would allow themselves to be gouged a bit. At twenty cents, they might have paid it for a week or a month, but they would have been forced to find another supplier.

Healy: In other words, when you said eight cents, they accepted it? But what if they said, "Wait a minute, I can see five." Would that have been satisfactory?

President: I'd probably have tried for five and a half or six. But they squirmed, and I sensed that they were stuck and they blinked first.

Healy: What if they had come back to you and said two cents or a penny?

President: I can't tell you what . . . well I'd have laughed at them with a penny, because I find that a lot of times you can use kind of a benevolent laugh—like, nice try, but come on, we're two mature people talking. It's a good way to refuse something. If they came at me seriously at a lower level, I would probably indicate that I didn't see any way we could do it. But before I turn off the deal, I want to think it through. "Honestly, I just don't think we can do it." That would be a typical way that I would react. It holds the most options. Social styles are important in negotiation. I'm a driver, so I like to control results and I like to keep my options open. So my negotiating style tends to try to accommodate those personal needs that I have.

Healy: Did they have a sense in the beginning of this that you were the authority and could make the commitment, or did you have to go back and check in with someone.

President: Good question. For some reason, even though I was very young to fill the position, they didn't question my authority; I suppose the could have. They should have been more concerned about that, because historically the chemical industry doesn't give that authority at my level, if for no other reason than to keep their options open. They didn't try to go around me. I suspect that if they did, my boss would have cut them off at the knees, because he liked to have control. If he got personally involved, then he'd lose options. So, using me as his front man gave him an eleventh hour option. You know, "My young guy screwed it up. I'll put him aside and come in and work with you." He never had to do that, but he always had that option.

Gottlieb: There seems to be a lot of uncertainty, a sense of "winging it" in what you're saying. Are you comfortable with that?

President: Psychologically, I like to wing it. I work best in a high energy, unstructured way. So, I think in this instance, I was a particularly good person to have at

	the negotiating table. In a labor relations type negotiation, I'd be a horrible person to do it.
Gottlieb:	Where do you perceive the difference?
President:	Well, in labor negotiations you've got a lot of history to consider and a lot of precedence that you're setting for the future, and it's much more adversarial. In the situation we just discussed, these were people who wanted something and we had it. In the case of labor negotiation, if you have someone doing fly-by-the-seat-of-the-pants stuff that I was doing, you might set some long-term precedents that you couldn't live with. In the business deal situation, the worst thing that could have happened is that we dropped that deal and we were left no worse off than we started. So, I had very little downside risk and time was on our side.

KNOW YOUR COMMUNICATION STYLE

In the preceding interview, our negotiator was consciously aware of and repeatedly analyzed his own negotiation style. It is a good rule to follow that you know yourself first and then your competitor. Your basic communicating style is pervasive in all interpersonal situations. It sets the style with which you negotiate. The strongest measures found in psychological research suggest the existence of two extremely dominant dimensions—control and worth.

Control, as discussed in Chapter 3, comes in two varieties: (1) an internal locus of control where the real or perceived control or ability to determine outcomes of situations rests within the individual, and (2) an external locus of control where the real or perceived control or ability to determine outcomes of situations rests with fate or with others. These extremes provide the vertical axis for the Negotiation Interaction Model (see Figure 5.1).

The horizontal axis represents Understanding. Positively (to the right), it focuses on responsiveness, warmth, and concern for others and for the relationship underlying the negotiation process. Negatively (to the left), understanding diminishes to unresponsiveness and

Figure 5.1. Negotiation Interaction Model

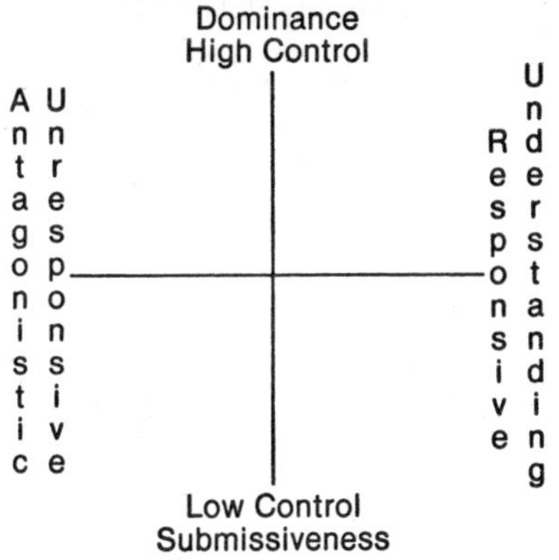

```
                    Dominance
                   High Control
                                         U
      A U                                n
      n n                              R d
      t r                              e e
      a e                              s r
      g s                              p s
      o p_____o t
      n o                              n a
      i n                              s n
      s s                              i d
      t i                              v i
      i v                              e n
      c e                                g
                    Low Control
                   Submissiveness
```

antagonism. It is characterized by a lack of concern for the needs of others, hostility, and a rejection of the underlying relationship. The vertical axis represents the level of dominance or submissiveness in the negotiation process. The top-most portion is high control, the lower-most portion is low control.

Figure 5.2 reveals the four types of negotiation styles (S): Collaborator (S1), Accommodator (S2). Avoider (S3), and Competitor (S4), and shows us where those styles are oriented in relation to understanding versus antagonism as well as dominance versus submissiveness. Each has its inherent weaknesses and strengths, depending on the context and dynamics of any negotiation situation. Few people are rigidly one type or another. In fact, in virtually every negotiation, people exhibit a combination of these behaviors. Which behavior becomes dominant depends on many factors:

Perceived or real risk or reward potential

Time pressure

Popularity or disfavor of the issue under consideration

Style of the negotiators

Number of other people involved in or affected by the negotiation

Skill levels of the negotiators, and

Long- and short-term impact of the negotiated situation.

The outcome of any negotiation is determined by a large number of factors that includes substantive, personal, and relationship issues.

Figure 5.2. Negotiation Interaction Model: Behaviors/Orientation

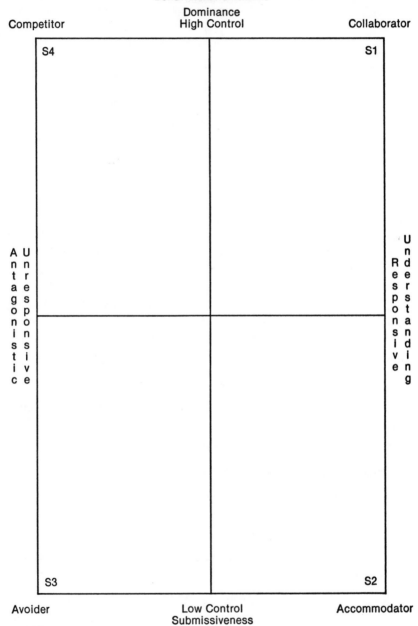

The chemistry among the negotiators cannot be underestimated as a factor that strongly influences the results. We have conducted ongoing research with groups of individuals having similar backgrounds and skills who are given the same negotiation scenario to role play. The extraordinary range of outcomes is largely attributed to the interaction of the preceding factors, since all parties are working with the same factual input.

The skilled negotiator is—to some degree—in control of the style he or she is using at any given moment in a negotiation. It is the context of the negotiation that dictates the appropriate style. One style may be on target for one negotiation, and completely wrong for another. Using Figure 5.2 as a backdrop, let's look at the assets and liabilities of each style.

Competitor (S4)

When decisive, quick action, which has the potential for unpopularity, is required (as in an emergency situation), S4s may be able to negotiate in their favor. However, the long-term results and fallout from one way, forced compliance may have extremely negative after effects. (See Figure 5.3.) S4 negotiators (power-oriented behavior) rarely involve others in the negotiating planning process and feel that they must decide and carry out the negotiation on their own. To do otherwise, in their view, would be a sign of weakness.

In the actual negotiating situation, S4s will tend to overcontrol and dominate the conversation. Or, as was discussed in Chapter 3 they tend to be controllers when it comes to setting the communication rules. Some specific or overt statements about who is calling the shots will be made. The S4 individual will be highly reluctant to give up any control in the negotiation process including who is there, concessions, timing, and so forth. The negotiating style will be one of pushing, demanding, and making flat assertions.

The S4 negotiator may often be surrounded by "yes" people who have found it unwise to disagree. Therefore, they have been blocked off from some potentially important information.

Avoider (S3)

S3 negotiators (status-quo-oriented behavior) avoid personal contact to the extent possible and often prefer to interact in the deal through bid requests, preferably blind bid submissions. (See Figure 5.4.) S3s

Figure 5.3. Negotiation Interaction Model: Competitor (S4)

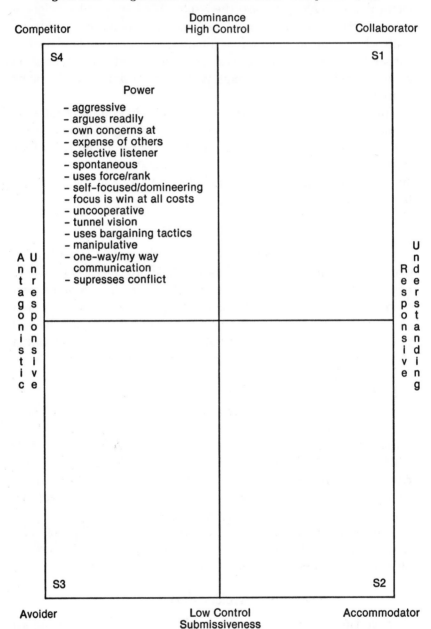

are perhaps the hardest to read since their tendency to withdraw and remain aloof from personal involvements is very high. People who exhibit S3 behavior often have lower power positions and are sometimes frustrated trying to get their own way. They are reluctant to change and often hide behind policies that support the status quo. They often use historical precedence as the required way of doing business.

They may prefer to send out detailed requests for proposals including full specifications on trivial items and receive back detailed proposals from interested bidders. They would then spend whatever time necessary to review these in depth, and finally choose the safest proposal. In this way they take the least amount of risk or exposure in terms of their own job. In the face of conflict, they will also withdraw or tend to postpone it indefinitely.

Avoidant behavior can be useful when attempting to let disagreeing parties cool down in an attempt to reduce tension and regain perspective. The collaborator (S1) controls the time out, and calls it in response to the group's need to cool down. Whereas, the S3 uses it as a way to get out of conflict and escape.

S3s are sometimes not involved in negotiations—not because they are unwilling, which they are—but because organizational members have stopped asking for their opinions and input. When planning for a negotiation they rely heavily on detailed input from their own superiors before any outside exposure is ventured. They tend to function in a role of information collectors who will pass on retrieved data for others to act on.

When organizing negotiation situations, they prefer to follow detailed procedures and policies, and are extremely reluctant to deviate from tested or established norms. Any control that they attempt to exert takes the form of sticking to the procedure established. They may be uncomfortable in free-form negotiations where there is little preapproved structure. They tend to be low-influence individuals with a pessimistic view toward the outcome of a negotiation. People are forced to deal with them because of policies that have been set up to keep them involved. The other three types of negotiators (S1s, S2s, and S4s) would generally prefer not to have to deal with an S3.

Accommodator (S2)

Accommodators have a high need to involve (and overinvolve) virtually everyone affected by the outcome of a negotiated situation. (See

Figure 5.4. Negotiation Interaction Model: Avoider (S3)

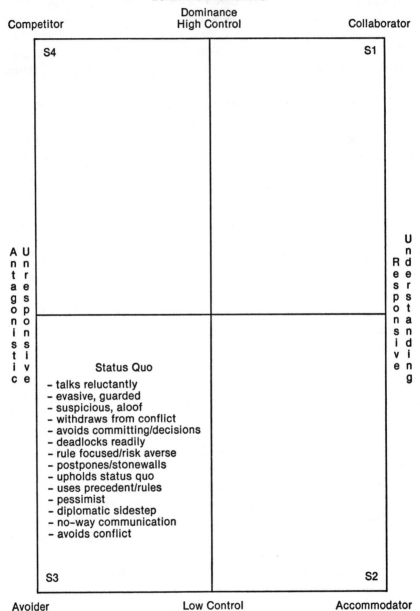

Behaviors/Orientations

Dominance
High Control

Competitor   Collaborator

S4   S1

A U
n n
t r
a e
g s
o p
n o
i n
s s
t i
i v   Status Quo
c e
        – talks reluctantly
        – evasive, guarded
        – suspicious, aloof
        – withdraws from conflict
        – avoids committing/decisions
        – deadlocks readily
        – rule focused/risk averse
        – postpones/stonewalls
        – upholds status quo
        – uses precedent/rules
        – pessimist
        – diplomatic sidestep
        – no-way communication
        – avoids conflict

U
n
R d
e e
s r
p s
o t
n a
s n
i d
v i
e n
g

S3   S2

Avoider   Low Control   Accommodator
                           Submissiveness

74

Figure 5.5.) They will be among the first to make popular concessions in the hope of winning future favors, and put the relationship ahead of winning and/or following an unpopular policy. An S2's preparation and organization for negotiation tend to be loose and focused on generating good will. (They think: "If people like me and feel good about the negotiation, I will end up with a good deal.") Many times, they allow and prefer others to control the situation, and as negotiators they spend an inordinate amount of time on relationship building. In the face of conflict they will tend to smooth things over and sometimes make concessions to gain peace.

The S2 negotiator (friendship-oriented behavior) tends to ramble on about issues and often appears to agree with just about everyone. The S2 is often deferent to the interests and roles of others, resulting in reduced credibility, influence, respect, and recognition. They are, however, pleasant and likable. When forced to decide among vendors, they try to avoid offending by spreading the business around to keep everyone happy and involved.

Collaborator (S1)

The collaborator is driven by finding a solution that is pragmatic and addresses both the substantive or factual issues at hand as well as building relationships for long-term pay back. (See Figure 5.6.) They carefully consider who else should be involved in the decision, and share the power according to the needs of the situation.

S1 negotiators (results-oriented behavior) will consult with and ask for the opinions of others who may be functional experts or staff members and are not afraid to share the negotiating table with other people on the team. They believe that policies and procedures exist to be adhered to as long as they are functional, but should change when they do not add value to the situation.

The S1 negotiator can be as strong and as dominant as the S4, but the control is focused on overcoming the problem, not the other negotiators. The S1 is able to merge insights from different people on their own negotiating team, as well as from the other side, and is adept at gaining commitment to integrative solutions where the concerns of both parties can be reconciled.

If conflict exits or hard feelings evolve during the process, the S1 negotiator can confront them constructively. The S1 style may require a longer time because of the collaborative nature of the approach. But,

Figure 5.5. Negotiation Interaction Model: Accommodator (S2)

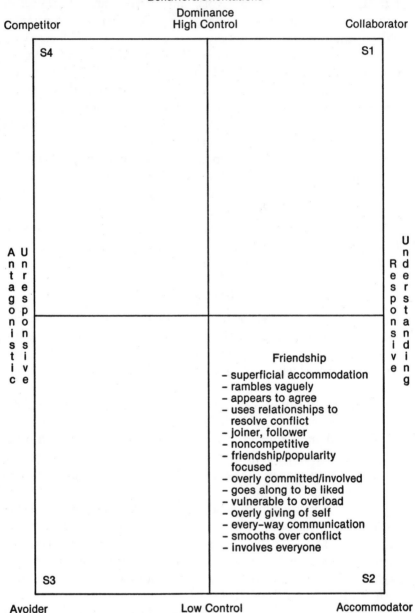

Behaviors/Orientations

Dominance
High Control

Competitor   Collaborator

S4   S1

A U   U
n n   n
t r   R   d
a e   e   e
g s   s   r
o p   p   s
n o   o   t
i n   n   a
s s   s   n
t i   Friendship   i   d
i v   v   i
c e   – superficial accommodation e   n
                                    – rambles vaguely   g
                                    – appears to agree
                                    – uses relationships to
                                      resolve conflict
                                    – joiner, follower
                                    – noncompetitive
                                    – friendship/popularity
                                      focused
                                    – overly committed/involved
                                    – goes along to be liked
                                    – vulnerable to overload
                                    – overly giving of self
                                    – every–way communication
                                    – smooths over conflict
                                    – involves everyone

S3   S2

Avoider   Low Control   Accommodator
                                    Submissiveness

Figure 5.6. Negotiation Interaction Model: Collaborator (S1)

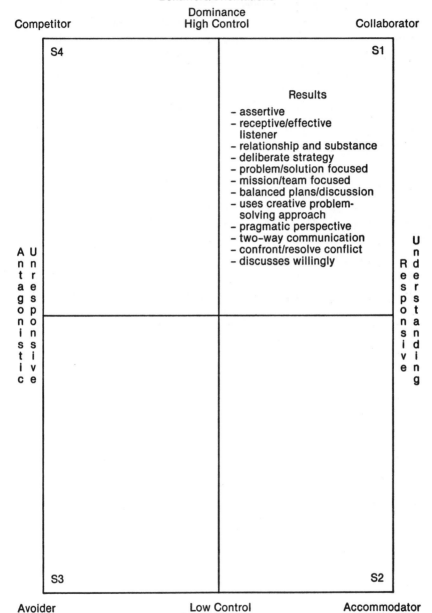

77

the satisfaction with relationships and substantive issues is most often greater than with other styles.

The realities of negotiation dictate that there is not always as much time as one would want to work collaboratively through all of the issues. Therefore, when urgent or immediate decisions are required, the S1 person may need to be more direct and less collaborative, and shift the style toward S4 while still keeping to the responsive side of the scale. By maintaining a balance of control and responsiveness, the solutions arrived at will probably be more satisfactory in a long-term relationship.

BENEFITS AND LIABILITIES OF STYLE

The four interpersonal negotiating styles (Figure 5.7) are mediated by the situation, and each has some inherent benefits and liabilities.

The S4 Negotiating Style

Fear of "shooting the messenger" often reduces the S4's access to important information. This may also lead the S4 to the feeling of being set up, when entering the negotiation without a critical piece of information. Yet, everything the high S4 negotiator does precludes others from offering suggestions or alternatives; S4s generally appear to want to do it their way. The characteristics of an S4 are particularly difficult for S3s and S2s to deal with.

In an organizational setting, subordinates may fear admitting uncertainties and engage in some S4 play acting on their own. They act more forceful or convinced of a course of action than they really are. People with very low control tendencies can often feel powerless—a severe detriment in a negotiation.

A skilled negotiator is well aware of his or her actual power in a negotiation. Positioning yourself as having more power than you really have may work against you in negotiating. However, feeling that you are powerless restricts your influence on others. The inability to take a firm stand even when there is an explicit need to do so can diminish personal credibility. Low S4 control can cause continual rescheduling and postponing of decisions on negotiating circumstances.

The S3 Negotiating Style

An S3s may avoid confronting issues in favor of generating new alternatives that produce less conflict. When negotiating with an S3,

Figure 5.7. Negotiation Interaction Model: Competitor (S4), Avoider (S3), Accommodator (S2), and Collaborator (S1)

Behaviors/Orientations

Dominance
High Control

Competitor   Collaborator

S4	S1
Power	**Results**
– aggressive	– assertive
– argues readily	– receptive/effective
– own concerns at	listener
expense of others	– relationship and substance
– selective listener	– deliberate strategy
– spontaneous	– problem/solution focused
– uses force/rank	– mission/team focused
– self–focused/domineering	– balanced plans/discussion
– focus is win at all costs	– uses creative problem-
– uncooperative	solving approach
– tunnel vision	– pragmatic perspective
– uses bargaining tactics	– two-way communication
– manipulative	– confront/resolve conflict
– one-way/my way	– discusses willingly
communication	
– supresses conflict	
Status Quo	**Friendship**
– talks reluctantly	– superficial accommodation
– evasive, guarded	– rambles vaguely
– suspicious, aloof	– appears to agree
– withdraws from conflict	– uses relationships to
– avoids committing/decisions	resolve conflict
– deadlocks readily	– joiner, follower
– rule focused/risk averse	– noncompetitive
– postpones/stonewalls	– friendship/popularity
– upholds status quo	focused
– uses precedent/rules	– overly committed/involved
– pessimist	– goes along to be liked
– diplomatic sidestep	– vulnerable to overload
– no-way communication	– overly giving of self
– avoids conflict	– every-way communication
	– smooths over conflict
	– involves everyone
S3	S2

Antagonistice Unresponsonsive
Responsive Understanding

Avoider   Accommodator

Low Control
Submissiveness

79

the process may be over but you might not know it! When confronted, S3s will usually provide one or several unverifiable policy reasons for their actions. Extreme S3 tendencies may be indicative of accumulated frustration over past difficulties in changing policies or otherwise influencing circumstances that were apparently outside their control. These may include significant industry trends, competitive price cutting, company policy, and so on.

S3 behavior may be effective when there is the potential for damage that would result from confronting particular situations or people. Avoiding or sidestepping an issue can be appropriate when the issue is unimportant. Withdrawing in order to allow people to cool down and reduce tension may be a productive, temporary solution. When it is necessary to gather more information and defer immediate action, S3 behavior may be more appropriate than direct action and confrontation. A popular S3 response is to defer to others who are somewhat more technically capable of handling or resolving the conflict, but more willing to take the risk. S3s are often advisors rather than decision makers. Negotiators with a good amount of S3 tendencies are often difficult for other negotiators to read and may cause feelings of suspicion or hostility.

S3s have a somewhat compulsive, protective nature that may result in their being overwhelmed by details. Obsessing with data, rules, and policy compliance in an attempt to minimize risk can result in creating their own paperwork nightmare. The S3 sees specific policies and procedures as reasons for not acting to resolve a negotiating difference. Policy and procedure compliance is the goal, not solving the problem. A good deal of this avoidance behavior can result in coordination difficulties. S3s can be frustrating because people do not know where the S3 stands on particular issues. This gives rise to speculation that this may be a deliberate ploy on the part of the S3 to force others to make a decision and thus insulate the S3 from the risk.

The S2 Negotiating Style

Falling back on the relationship and friendship may help in some tense situations, or where it is realized that the negotiator has made a factual error. S2s may personalize the situation. Moving too far toward relationship dependence may yield control and allow the negotiator to be perceived as vulnerable. Conversely, people who need to be perceived as perfect can sometimes make ideal targets for others who feel the need to tear them down or manipulate them.

S2 negotiating style may also be appropriate when a particular issue is apparently much more important to one negotiator than it is to the other. Providing a concession in a situation such as this may in fact put you in a good position to seek a reciprocal concession. However, as discussed earlier, the request for this reciprocity should be made before or relatively close to agreeing to the other person's concession. Otherwise, it sets up the scenario of the other person taking advantage of the S2's accommodating style by demanding a series of concessions without any reciprocity.

S2's accommodating behavior may also be helpful as a gesture of good will in certain situations, particularly when there is relatively little risk or cost to the S2. It is preferred, however, that prior to making the good will gesture or concession, the value or relative importance of the concession be established. Otherwise, later in the negotiation it will be difficult to agree on or establish values for a concession which was readily thrown in as being "no problem."

High accommodation styles may provide more opportunities to get to know your competition in a less threatening atmosphere. S2 behavior in negotiating situations may be adopted when continued competition or attempts to control the situation would only damage your case for more significant issues. This style can also be useful when trying to avoid further disruptions and when preserving the relationship is especially important for the longer term.

Too much accommodation (S2) may reinforce the perception of low power. This can serve to undermine personal impact and credibility. It also diminishes the impact that any valid points made in a negotiation would normally have. Dealing with high S2s can be very frustrating for people with more S1 or S4 tendencies. The apparent continual agreement and deferring of decisions often evokes the response, "We can never seem to get an answer from him."

The S1 Negotiating Style

In general, this style of negotiating is preferred to all the others. It is particularly effective when the relative risks are high and the time pressures are reasonable. There is a willingness to include others to arrive at a decision that is good for everyone. The involvement of others is used to reinforce or gain commitment. Collaboration is helpful to refine solutions based on the collective input of others affected by the negotiation settlement. It is an effective way to confront conflict or hard feelings which may have been interfering with the negotiation process. S2, S3, and S4 relationships may have to be addressed before substantive issues can be resolved.

Extremely high S1 scorers[1] may spend too much time involving others in relatively minor decisions which could in fact be dispensed with quite readily. The key to using collaborative behavior is in determining how much collaboration a particular situation needs. Too much collaboration can be a detriment.

Too much collaboration may in fact lead to "groupthink" or "risky shift"—increasing the comfort level of a decision by spreading the risk among more people. Collaboration is counterproductive if it is used (as in S2) as a way of diffusing decision making, minimizing risk acceptance or postponing action. If collaborative behaviors fail, it may be because other people feel that what they are experiencing is more of an S4 manipulation with the pretense of involvement. In fact, experience shows that once a person has already made up his or her mind on a negotiation issue, his or her involvement behavior is S4, manipulation, not S1, collaboration and openness.

People with very low S1 styles may find it difficult to accept differences or conflict as opportunities. One S1 person put conflict in a healthy perspective: "If we all agree on something, some of us must be redundant." A moderate amount of disagreement or differing opinions on an issue may cause constructive and creative examination of more options than would have been identified if everyone agreed.

ANTICIPATING AND DEALING WITH STYLE INTERACTIONS

S4-S3 Negotiations

An S4 negotiator against an S3 negotiator will often result in relatively short sessions with one side clearly being the more vocal, pushy, direct, and demanding. (See Figure 5.8.) That would be the S4 style. S3s would probably react with a fair amount of evasiveness, and a noncommittal attitude. They would try to withdraw and hide behind a blind bid situation or request a detailed proposal.

Figure 5.8. Negotiation Interaction Model: Competitor (S4) and Avoider (S3)

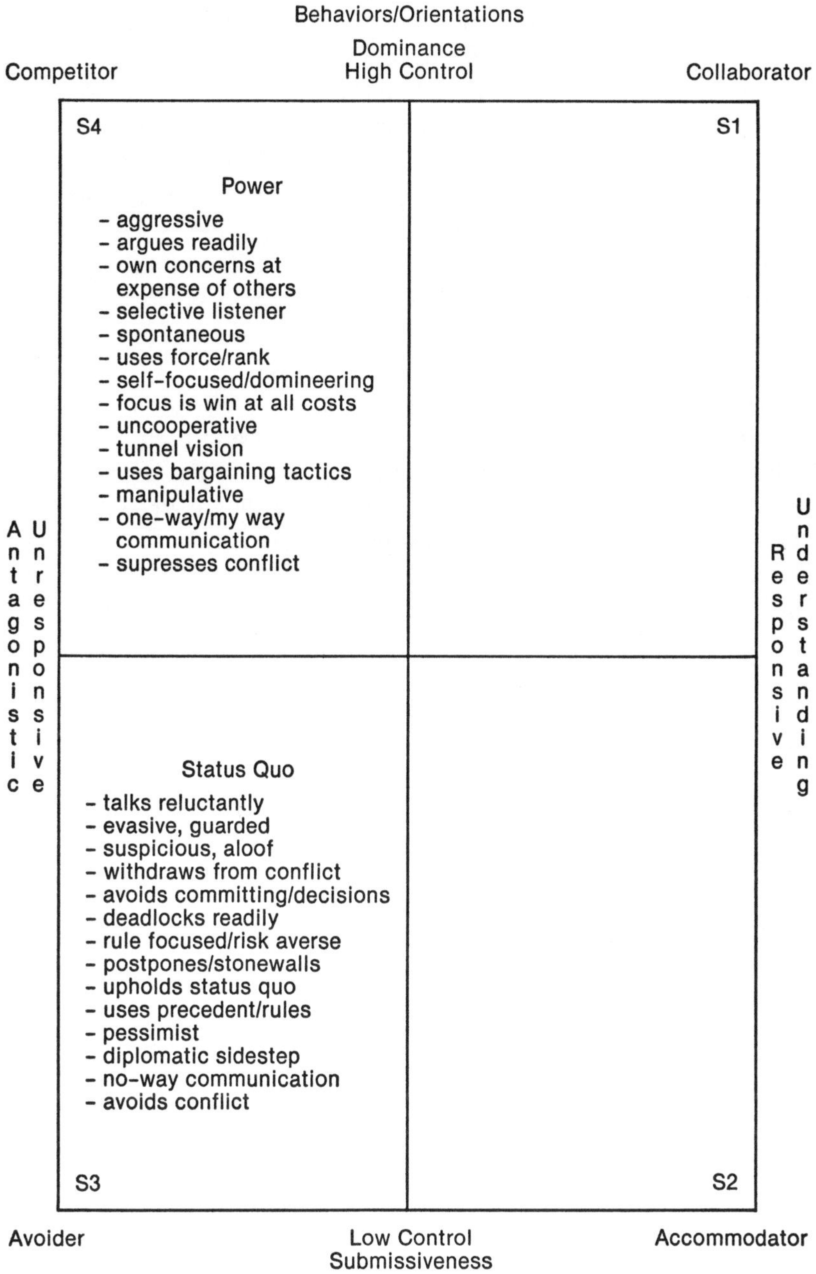

Behaviors/Orientations

Dominance
High Control

Competitor		Collaborator

S4		**S1**
Power		
– aggressive		
– argues readily		
– own concerns at expense of others		
– selective listener		
– spontaneous		
– uses force/rank		
– self-focused/domineering		
– focus is win at all costs		
– uncooperative		
– tunnel vision		
– uses bargaining tactics		
– manipulative		
– one-way/my way communication		
– supresses conflict		
Status Quo		
– talks reluctantly		
– evasive, guarded		
– suspicious, aloof		
– withdraws from conflict		
– avoids committing/decisions		
– deadlocks readily		
– rule focused/risk averse		
– postpones/stonewalls		
– upholds status quo		
– uses precedent/rules		
– pessimist		
– diplomatic sidestep		
– no-way communication		
– avoids conflict		
S3		**S2**

A n t a g o n i s t i c e — U n r e s p o n s i v e

R e s p o n s i v e — U n d e r s t a n d i n g

Avoider		Accommodator

Low Control
Submissiveness

83

The S3 confronted by a S4 will attempt to use historical precedents and procedures as a defensive posture to the aggressive and often perceived abrasive style of the S4. S4s will often present predetermined solutions, and the S3 response will be to find personal or company guidelines that will defend against the S4's assertions.

An S3 can be rather quickly intimidated by an S4. S3s are masters at politics and are ingenious at creating road blocks and deadlocks which can indefinitely hold up any negotiation they view as a threat. The S3 is adept at diplomatically sidestepping issues raised by S4s as well as avoiding personal confrontation, deferring conflict, and transferring blame. They will rarely initiate conflict but are ready with reasons why something should not or cannot be done. They may have thick files insulating them from S4 demands.

The S3 is generally able to then terminate or indefinitely deadlock the negotiation, having made his or her point and then withdrawn. The S4 is unlikely to be able to get access again to the S3, since they can successfully surround themselves with policies, procedures and bureaucracy, or just personal evasions of contact.

S4s who deal with S3s and S2s very often have little regard for them as individuals. The S4 has little tolerance or time to meet the S2's relationship needs and the S4 is equally put off by the S3's adherence to policies and procedures. The S4 would rather create whatever policies and procedures they need to achieve their goals and are willing to bend or break whatever rules appear to be creating roadblocks for them.

S4-S2 Negotiations

A S4 can readily overwhelm the happy-go-lucky accommodator. The S2 negotiator may quickly submit to the raging S4, as a way to gain friendship. (See Figure 5.9.) The S2 may allow the other side to gain full disclosure of the S2's key issues without the need for reciprocal disclosure. An S2 voices apparent agreement with many of the points made, not wanting to create conflict or animosity. Idealistically, the S2 feels that if the other party "likes me" he'll do O.K.

In response to the demands the S4 makes on the S2, the S2 negotiator will ramble on vaguely and often at length about marginally related situations in an attempt to build a relationship. This person seeks the establishment of a relationship, but it is unlikely since the S4 will view the S2 as a weak person. The S2 will often go along and

Figure 5.9. Negotiation Interaction Model: Competitor (S4) and Accommodator (S2)

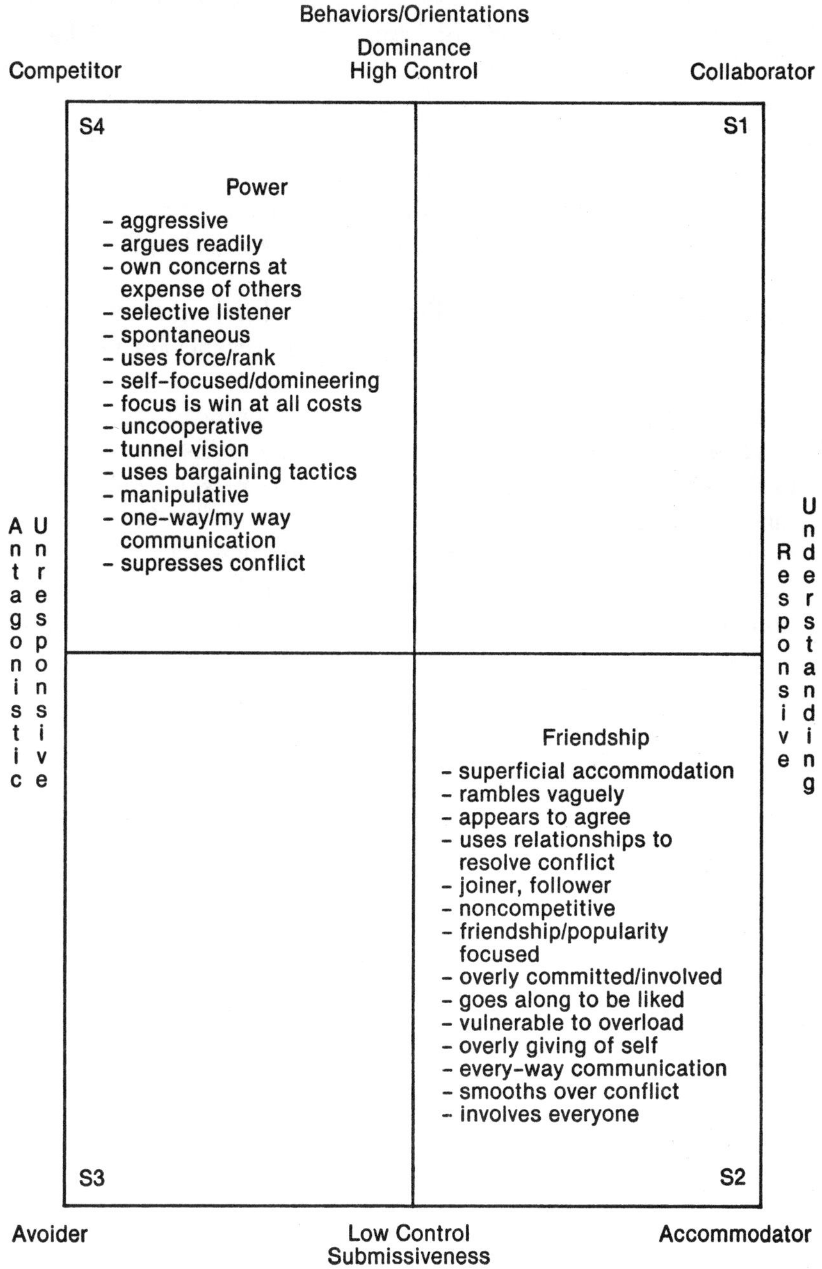

Behaviors/Orientations
Dominance
High Control

Competitor   Collaborator

S4	S1
Power - aggressive - argues readily - own concerns at expense of others - selective listener - spontaneous - uses force/rank - self-focused/domineering - focus is win at all costs - uncooperative - tunnel vision - uses bargaining tactics - manipulative - one-way/my way communication - supresses conflict	
	Friendship - superficial accommodation - rambles vaguely - appears to agree - uses relationships to resolve conflict - joiner, follower - noncompetitive - friendship/popularity focused - overly committed/involved - goes along to be liked - vulnerable to overload - overly giving of self - every-way communication - smooths over conflict - involves everyone
S3	S2

Antagonistic — Unresponsive (left side)

Understanding — Responsive (right side)

Avoider   Accommodator

Low Control
Submissiveness

85

sometimes make early concessions as a strategy to become liked by the S4. The S2 lacks the control needed to initiate reciprocal concessions.

One typical response in this situation is for the S2 to take the forcefully delivered position of the S4 and run it by everyone even remotely involved in making the decision. The S2 negotiator can, however, be relatively effective in smoothing over conflicts. However, the S2 often lacks the respect of the more dominant party that is necessary to achieve any real conflict resolution. The reason presented to the S4 for rejection of a deal or request is usually along the lines of, ". . . they wouldn't go for it."

An S2 negotiator who is bullied or coerced into agreeing to terms pushed by an S4 negotiator may, because of weakness or need to be liked, accept the terms and later feel very abused and/or dissatisfied with the accepted terms. They may lie in wait for the next opportunity to get even. The S2 who is being pushed by an S4 negotiator will likely either become more withdrawn as the pressure increases, or superficially appear to agree to the imposed agreement. In some cases, S2s may overact and strike back at the S4 with their own S4 behavior, but later refocus on the relationship. This usually results in an explosion of tempers, because the S4 then retaliates with power and assertiveness, and without any remorse for the injured relationship to moderate the response.

S4-S1 Negotiations

The S4-S1 negotiation can be somewhat frustrating for an S4 negotiator. (See Figure 5.10.) Flat assertions and demands are not weakly accepted or counterargued, rather they are probed with insight to find out underlying basis for the assertions and rationale for the S4 demands. In effect, the S4 is dealing with someone equally dominant but with a better focus on the problems and issues, rather than defending hard positions.

The S1 collaborator can gain the respect of the S4 by meeting each point head-on with key issues, a respect lacking with S4-S3 as well as S4-S2 negotiations. The key difference here, between S4 and S1, is the S4's focus on a predetermined position and the S1's focus on the problem or situation. The S1 is likely to force a more creative solution based on redirecting the insight and energy of the S4 toward a problem-solving activity and away from the predetermined solution. The S1 is capable of direct and strong confrontation, but in a positive and constructive manner.

Figure 5.10. Negotiation Interaction Model: Competitor (S4) and Collaborator (S1)

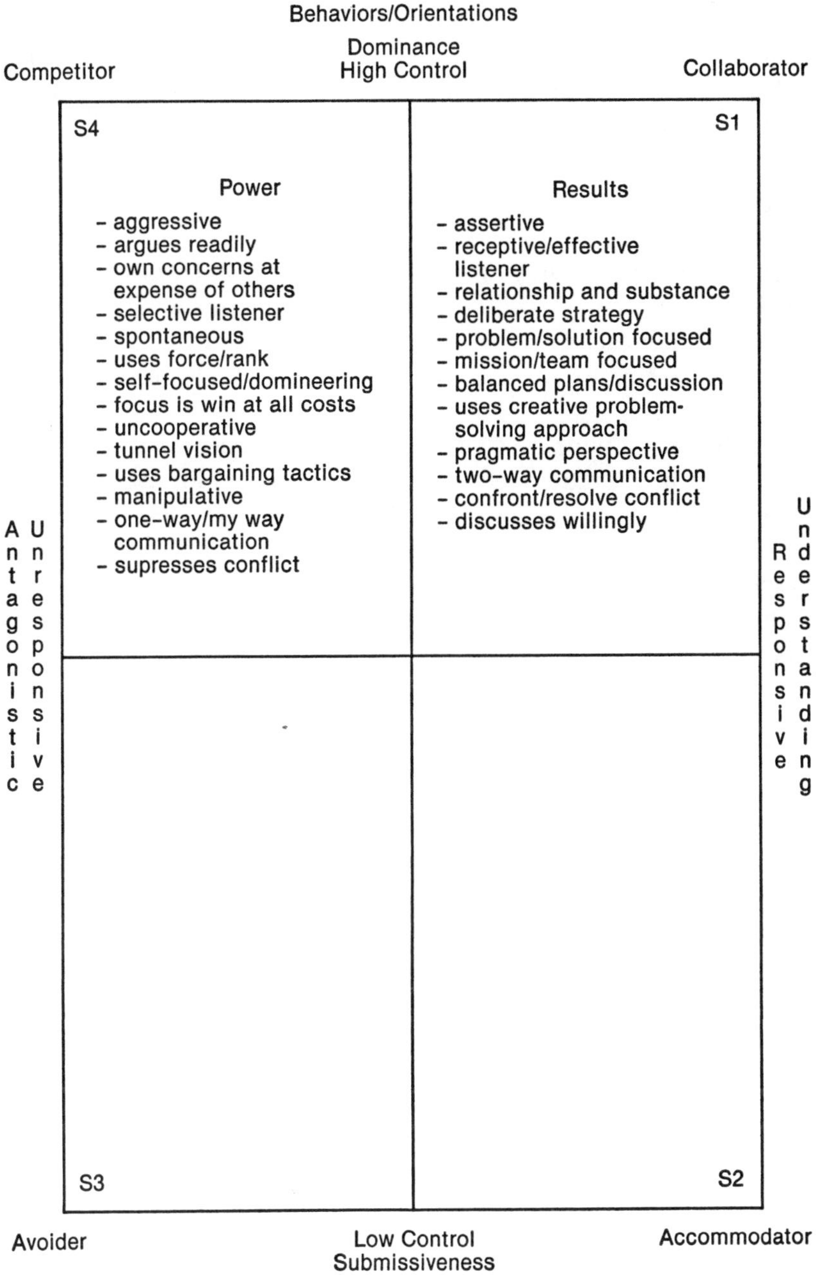

Behaviors/Orientations

Dominance
High Control

Competitor

Collaborator

S4		S1

Power

- aggressive
- argues readily
- own concerns at
  expense of others
- selective listener
- spontaneous
- uses force/rank
- self-focused/domineering
- focus is win at all costs
- uncooperative
- tunnel vision
- uses bargaining tactics
- manipulative
- one-way/my way
  communication
- supresses conflict

Results

- assertive
- receptive/effective
  listener
- relationship and substance
- deliberate strategy
- problem/solution focused
- mission/team focused
- balanced plans/discussion
- uses creative problem-
  solving approach
- pragmatic perspective
- two-way communication
- confront/resolve conflict
- discusses willingly

Antagonistic   Unresponsive

Unresponsive   Understanding

S3		S2

Avoider

Low Control
Submissiveness

Accommodator

87

The S1 negotiator may be able to skillfully use a deliberate time out (not a S3 withdrawal) to cool off the S4 during the course of the negotiation. The S1 will use this move to uncover additional facts and information to support the case, as well as to allow the S4 to reconsider established positions that may have been developed hastily.

S3-S3 Negotiations

The S3-S3 negotiation appears strained from the beginning. (See Figure 5.4.) Both parties provide information very reluctantly and are very committed to their own internal or personal procedures and guidelines. Both might well be content with a paper shuffling negotiation in which each party submits to each other in turn their list of required information, a date for a response, and detailed specifications.

These negotiations are characterized by a high degree of suspiciousness, with both parties ready to deadlock at any point over noncompliance with the other's request. Conflict, if it occurs, is likely to result in a lack of communication and deadlock. The occurrence of something during the course of the negotiation not covered by their comfortable rules and procedures can create a significant delay in procedures. In all likelihood, neither party will be willing to make a commitment on any given issue without identifying others in their hierarchy to accept the risk or make a decision.

These negotiations often lack creativity and spontaneity, which sometimes results in a more satisfactory negotiation given each party's ability to at least consider the other party's position. It is almost a certainty that neither party really enjoys the process of negotiating and would just as soon see this activity carried on by someone else. Communication is usually minimal, and what does exist is formal and carefully edited.

Both sides are content with maintaining the status quo. They would rather have a safe agreement than one involving any increment of risk or innovation which they perceive as potentially jeopardizing their safety and status quo.

S3-S2 Negotiations

Negotiations between S3 and S2 styles are often exercises in frustration. (See Figure 5.11.) While the S3 is extremely guarded and

Figure 5.11. Negotiation Interaction Model: Avoider (S3) and Accommodator (S2)

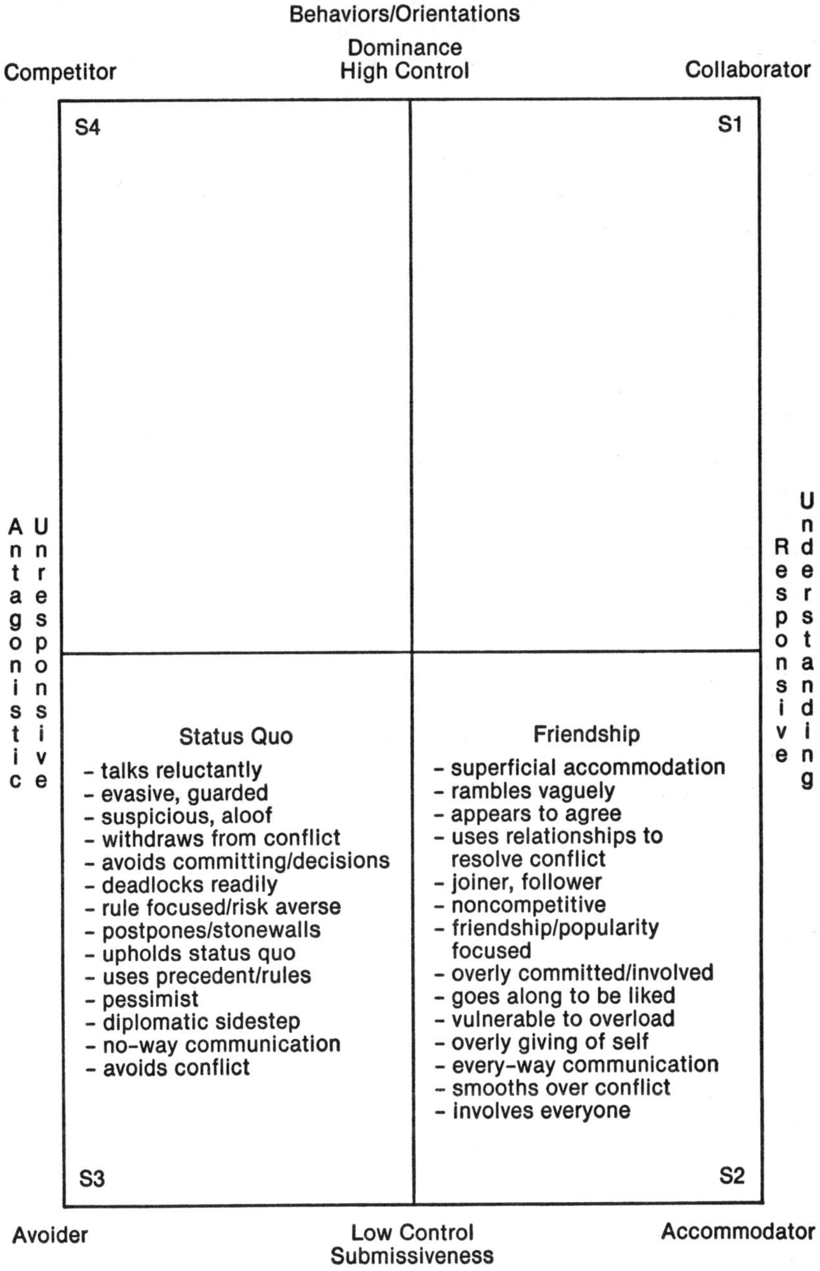

Behaviors/Orientations

Dominance
High Control

Competitor   Collaborator

S4	S1

Antagonistic   Unresponsive

Responsive   Understanding

Status Quo

– talks reluctantly
– evasive, guarded
– suspicious, aloof
– withdraws from conflict
– avoids committing/decisions
– deadlocks readily
– rule focused/risk averse
– postpones/stonewalls
– upholds status quo
– uses precedent/rules
– pessimist
– diplomatic sidestep
– no–way communication
– avoids conflict

Friendship

– superficial accommodation
– rambles vaguely
– appears to agree
– uses relationships to
   resolve conflict
– joiner, follower
– noncompetitive
– friendship/popularity
   focused
– overly committed/involved
– goes along to be liked
– vulnerable to overload
– overly giving of self
– every–way communication
– smooths over conflict
– involves everyone

S3   S2

Avoider   Low Control   Accommodator
                 Submissiveness

89

reluctant to communicate and prefers to avoid interaction, the S2 negotiator is driven in exactly the opposite direction; he would prefer to talk an issue to death and follow a relatively loose structure. After all, if it makes us happy, it should be acceptable. The S3 negotiator will view as suspicious the S2's friendship overtures. The S2 will see the S3's lack of involvement as distressing and potentially distrustful. The S2 negotiator will then become frustrated by the lack of relationship interest on the part of the S3 negotiator, but will not confront the S3 for fear that "he may not like me." Negotiations between S2s and S3s are likely to be lengthy because their personal needs are at odds. That is, S2s will seek to build a relationship with an S3 person; however, the S3's goal is to avoid interpersonal relationships and remain aloof in negotiations. An S2 would rather come out and talk about the issues while the S3 would rather have you send a memo regarding your position.

An S3-S2 negotiated agreement can often result in dissatisfaction for both parties. The S3 may never fully accept the relationship needs of the S2; in future negotiations, the S3 will probably try to create ways to avoid further contact with this individual. However, the S2 negotiator may never fully appreciate the need to deal again with the S3 because the S2's relationship needs were never met during the negotiation—even if a good agreement was achieved. The S2 may be driven to seek an alternative in the next negotiation which will allow him or her to get the same substantive issues received with the S3 but with an individual who could also meet his or her inherent S2 relationship needs.

S2-S2 Negotiations

The S2-S2 negotiations are likely to be the longest of all. (See Figure 5.5.) They may not result in any agreement, but a great friendship is likely to evolve. Both sides will freely express their thoughts, feelings, and concerns and readily be willing to listen to the thoughts, feelings, and concerns of the other party. However, with all of the concern placed on the relationship, often little progress is made on the substantive issues. Many time-consuming lunches and dinners may be invested in a relationship which has little long-term probability of fulfilling the substantive needs of either party. However, they may have a great time in the process.

Substantive issues are dealt with by providing mutual concessions. These concessions may ultimately be impossible to live up to. If they are required to live up to them, the result of the agreement may well be one of frustration and bitterness. S2-S2 negotiators may be reluctant to strain the relationship with the issue at hand, and the negotiation of substantive issues takes a backseat to friendship issues.

Both S2 negotiators may feel a compulsion to involve numerous other individuals from their organizations, each of whom may take their respective toll on the progress of negotiations. S2s will have great difficulty making a decision that they feel will be perceived as unfriendly or threatening, even if it is the only workable decision to make.

S1-S3 Negotiations

While the S3 negotiators may clearly prefer to withdraw and avoid dealing with issues openly, the S1 collaborator would be skillful at involving and drawing out the S3 with appropriate questioning and listening skills. (See Figure 5.12.) The S1 should probe the positions, needs, fears, concerns, and so forth held by the S3 negotiator using patience and assurance.

The S1 is dominant enough to continue to press for clarification of evasiveness in response to the issues, but not to the point of raising road-blocking, suspicious behavior on the part of the S3. The S1 will sense when the S3 has been pushed too far and is about to deadlock, and will take appropriate actions to keep the interaction going.

The S3 avoider may be reluctant to engage the S1 collaborator in conversation around the issues. However, the S1 approach is not as threatening as the S4 competitor's because the focus is directed at resolving an issue not "getting my way."

S1s can sometimes persuade S3s to provide additional information to the extent that they are comfortable and have been given a good rationale for disclosing the information. The S1 negotiator, facing a conflict such as the withholding of critical information or unwillingness to engage in critical discussions, is able to confront the situation and work toward a satisfactory resolution. The S1 negotiator recognizes the risk avoidance inherent in the S3 negotiator. S1's pragmatic perspective allows him or her to be sensitive to this risk avoidance; this helps the S1 to push the S3 to the point of considering alternatives without overly threatening the S3's security.

Figure 5.12. Negotiation Interaction Model: Avoider (S3) and Collaborator (S1)

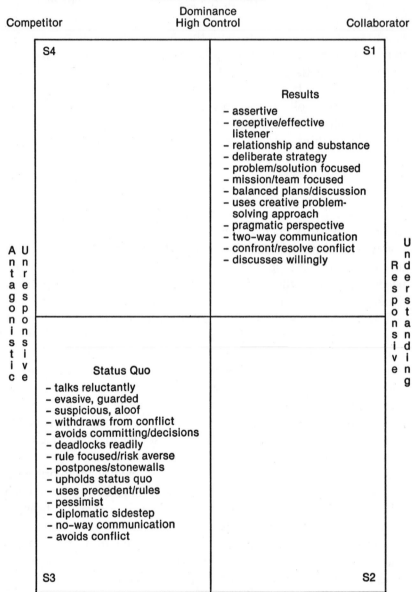

Behaviors/Orientations
Dominance
High Control

Competitor · · · Collaborator

S4 · · · S1

Results
- assertive
- receptive/effective listener
- relationship and substance
- deliberate strategy
- problem/solution focused
- mission/team focused
- balanced plans/discussion
- uses creative problem-solving approach
- pragmatic perspective
- two–way communication
- confront/resolve conflict
- discusses willingly

Antagonistic · Unresponsive · Responsive · Understanding

Status Quo
- talks reluctantly
- evasive, guarded
- suspicious, aloof
- withdraws from conflict
- avoids committing/decisions
- deadlocks readily
- rule focused/risk averse
- postpones/stonewalls
- upholds status quo
- uses precedent/rules
- pessimist
- diplomatic sidestep
- no–way communication
- avoids conflict

S3 · · · S2

Avoider · · · Accommodator
Low Control
Submissiveness

92

S1-S2 Negotiators

In the S1-S2 negotiation at least one party is able to remain focused on the substantive issues required of the negotiation. (See Figure 5.13.) While these negotiations can be friendly, the S1 will pull the negotiation in the direction of the issues that need to be resolved. This willingness to engage the S2 negotiator in conversation fulfills the S2's needs for friendship and a relationship. However, it also provides enough direction to focus the energy and discussion on the substantive issues.

The S2 finds the control or dominant behavior of the S1 less offensive than the S4 competitor, because the S1 is willing to demonstrate concern for the S2's position. This draws the two negotiators into a team, problem-solving focus. The S4's dominance or control is often overtly focused on unilaterally winning, while acknowledging very little concern for the relationship during the negotiation.

S1-S1 Negotiations

By now it should be evident that the S1-S1 negotiation is the most effective form of negotiation. (See Figure 5.6.) Both parties are clearly in control of their own positions. They are, however, willing to discuss and consider the relative positions of the other parties in an attempt to reconcile the various needs of each party. While the interaction is appropriately social, the relationship building does not dilute the concern for the substance of the negotiation.

S1-S1 negotiations tend to use creative problem-solving strategies for dealing with differences. They tend to be less emotional around the issues of personalities and can deal with significant differences in styles during the course of a negotiation. S1 negotiators are not too quick to compromise on significant issues, but rather focus on concepts such as expanding the pie, minimizing the risks, and maximizing the return of any given decision. They concede only when clear reasons are established or reasonable concessions in return are available. S1 negotiators avoid inappropriate stalling or deadlock situations, and rarely feel abused by the negotiation process.

S4-S4 Negotiations

Negotiations between two S4 style negotiators represent the classic battle of two strong positional bargainers. (See Figure 5.3.) The

Figure 5.13. Negotiation Interaction Model: Collaborator (S1) and Accommodator (S2)

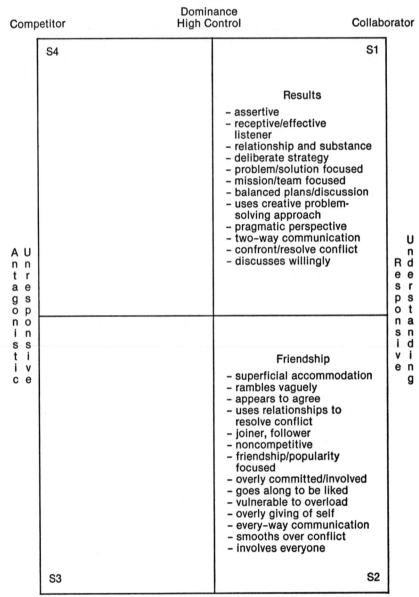

dialogue tends to be louder than most, with both sides launching numerous demands and flat assertions. Each campaigns strongly for his perceived needs without consideration for the needs of the other party. In fact, the needs of the other party are often dismissed, put down as unimportant, and viewed as threats to their own interests. If neither party attempts to take on the role of understander and respond to the other's needs, little progress can be expected. The success of S4 style is found in quick, though reluctant, compromise if the concessions are viewed as minor and not tarnishing the perception of winning the battle. More likely, the S4 negotiator will seek out others who can be dominated and forced to yield more quickly. In organizational hierarchies, negotiated solutions are often based on which S4 is in the superior position. And, as is true outside the company as well, many battles are won by S4s at the cost of losing the war.

IMPLICATIONS OF NEGOTIATION STYLES

Having looked at the various combinations of negotiation styles, it should be clear that the styles of the negotiator can significantly affect the real or perceived success and outcome of a given negotiation, even when all the factual information is identical. This has been seen numerous times in workshop research where identical factual data yield radically different outcomes. Satisfaction is sometimes highest in the solutions that are the most costly for both parties! Obviously, other needs are being met.

The Great House Purchase Saga

An individual we interviewed has recently concluded a house purchase in a shore community that had several very interesting twists to it which illustrate many of the negotiation points we have discussed. While this individual purchased several homes in the past for investment purposes, most of them were purchased closer to the asking price than he was willing to pay in this particular situation. The asking price on this particular property was $450,000.

There was no way the individual could or would pay that price. He had considered coming in with an offer of $400,000, but he didn't expect it to work. In a private person-to-person meeting with the seller, he offered $410,000—hoping that the person would agree. As soon as the offer was made, the other party did not react negatively or seem startled or put off in any way by the offer. Immediately, the buyer felt that he had probably offered too much. Shortly after the offer was made, he reduced the price to $400,000 alleging some defects in the house that he felt needed immediate repair. The seller felt that this was unacceptable and became angry. It is difficult to reduce an offer without enough reason, and this immediately started some personal conflict between the seller and buyer. This negotiation could have been a private deal with no real estate commissions involved, and would have netted the seller $400,000. Because of personal conflicts arising in the negotiation the deal fell apart.

A few weeks later, having listed the house at a 6 percent commission, the seller accepted an offer of $400,000 through a realtor. This meant that he would now net approximately $370,000 instead of the $400,000 he was offered directly. The bewildered and disappointed buyer in this situation tried to counter offer at $405,000 net to the seller, but to no avail because of the hostility that had already been created between the two parties. The deal at $400,000 with the realtor fell through. Our buyer learned about the collapse of the deal and made an offer that would net the seller approximately the same amount of money as he would have realized from the deal that just fell through. The offer was made, and accepted verbally. The contract, signed by the buyer, sat unsigned by the seller for five weeks.

It became clear during this two- to three-month period that the seller was, in fact, desperate to sell and get out of the property. It was ironic that the contract that was finally signed by the seller and returned after five weeks had significant legal and restrictive wordings that were prohibitive in the eyes of the buyer regarding inspection, title, mortgage, and other variables. Because of this the buyer canceled the contract—through his attorney—and had no further contact with the seller. At this point both the buyer and the seller have experienced a loss, one of the sale, and the other of the purchase.

A few weeks later, the buyer learned that the listing price had been reduced. To his amazement, the listing price had been reduced to $380,000. That is $20,000 less than the original offer price which he made at $400,000. It was a full $40,000 less if it sold at full asking price when you consider commissions. The seller could have walked away with $400,000. Now, under the best scenario he could only net approximately $360,000. The buyer was bewildered. After hearing the new listing price, the buyer learned that there was an offer pending at $370,000 and he quickly made an additional offer at full price $380,000 through the realtor. Because of the failure on two previous occasions to reach agreement, the offer—a full $10,000 above the other pending offer—was rejected with the comment that, "Should the buyer choose to still want the property, it is available to him for $400,000"—$20,000 above the current list price!

Emotion, conflict, and style can certainly influence decision making during negotiation. One could question the financial reasoning of such a counter offer given that the seller was in a position to gain at least $10,000 by the second offer, but the emotional need dominated the situation. However, the offer at $370,000 again fell through. This was brought to the attention of the buyer by a realtor who asked if he was still interested in the purchase of this property. The buyer indicated he would be, and offered $370,000—a price that would match the previous offer. The offer was presented to the seller who replied by saying, "You offered me $380,000 just last week." To this the buyer replied, "Yes, but that was when you had another offer and apparently you do not have another offer at this time."

At this point because of a dynamic created by style and emotional factors, the seller was now down to accepting an offer of $370,000 which would net him approximately $350,000—$50,000 less than the original offer proposed at $400,000 without commission.

The results of this particular negotiation do not typify anything other than this particular example. Many different outcomes could have been possible and a number of other options could have been created circumstantially. In some cases it is far better for the parties to deal directly, as was tried initially. This is something that we advocate in most negotiations. In this particular case, the needs of neither party were achieved as well as they could have been had both parties been more successful at negotiating their interests. While the buyer in this situation did pay $30,000 less than he might have paid originally, he missed part of the rental season in this shore community where the house was located. A better outcome could have been generated for both sides had the negotiation been conducted in a more collaborative, problem-solving (S1-S1) approach.

In this case, had one or preferably both negotiators adapted a more S1 style, it may have facilitated the decision to the betterment of both parties. This case demonstrates all four styles, and the way behaviors can shift during a negotiation. In one instance, when the decision or the contract was offered, one party resorted to an S4 negotiation style (i.e., take-it-or-leave-it), and the other party reverted to an S3 style (avoided dealing with the conflict). Both negotiators exhibited a fair amount of S2 behavior because they both appeared to agree with each other's terms, that is, until they were written and presented. Had both negotiators managed to use an S1 style, they may have been able to iron out the difficulties much sooner.

Therefore, prior to entering a negotiation it is critical that each negotiator have a very clear awareness of his or her predominant style, and seek information about the style of the other party. It is recommended that an individual should—in every case—behave in a S1 fashion. However, it is difficult to change a lifetime of behavior prior to a negotiation. While this is a reasonable long-term goal, it is perhaps more practical and immediately beneficial to at least anticipate the impact of your style and be aware of the possible influence that the style of others may have on your behavior.

If for example, you recognize that you tend to be more S4 and you happen to be negotiating with someone who you judge to be more S2 or S3, you need to be aware of what your dominant, hard driving, demand-oriented behavior might produce in these types of individuals. If, however, you know that you tend to avoid conflicts, much like the S2 or S3 negotiator, you may want to recognize that you will have a tendency to talk around the issue in the hopes of establishing a relationship and avoiding conflict while failing to attain your real substantive issues.

The key here is awareness. While you won't be able to immediately change your inner workings, you can produce necessary and appropriate behaviors that reflect more compatible styles as the need arises during negotiation. Controlling your style becomes part of your negotiation skills, along with other essential tools like planning, questioning, and responding appropriately to tactics.

We begin an understanding of style by first discovering the tendencies within ourselves. Sources include feedback which we solicit openly from others who negotiate with us either across the table or as part of our team, or who simply know us well. We often have a blind spot with regard to how others perceive our behavior.

Asking for feedback on our style must be approached nondefensively. Putting the respondent in an awkward position to tell us how they really experience us is likely to yield information about our negotiation style that is (1) of little value, or worse, (2) misleading. One would hope that the people we ask will not deliberately mislead us. However, if they happen to be S2 or S3 in style they may prefer not to give us the kind of feedback that we genuinely need to confront our less-than-effective behavioral style. If, however, the person that we ask for feedback from is predominantly S4, they may give us a whole lot more than we ever choose to deal with in a critical, but not necessarily constructive, manner. Another source of good feedback about our negotiation style can be obtained by audio or videotaped practice sessions in which we negotiate actual or simulated situations which are either upcoming or have happened in our past.

Given reasonably accurate input regarding our style, we can better plan how we will present and react to proposals, counterproposals, and specific tactics that occur during a negotiation session. The adjustment will not always be easy, but at least we have a place to begin. If, for example, a demand is made for a concession and our inclination is to want to shrug our shoulders and walk away from the situation, we must realize that what we are doing is avoiding the conflict. Knowing this may not make us want to deal with it, but at least we will be more aware of the impact of withdrawing from the situation. It is here that the strategies and guidelines for more effective negotiation should be engaged. In this particular case, our tendency to avoid and flee from a conflict situation should be responded to with some open questions. These questions will help us to better understand:

Why the person has positioned their demands the way they have

What they really hope to achieve by these demands

What other issues are important to them

Withdrawing from the situation only takes us out of the negotiation. It does not move us further along. Withdrawing and deadlocking in negotiations is different from the ability, real or perceived, to walk away from the situation. A skilled negotiator walks away from a bad deal, not from a conflict.

Throughout the negotiation it is critical that you recognize your style will vary considerably, depending on the factors at play during any given moment. We must start with every intention of performing in an S1 fashion throughout the negotiation. However, because of certain personal characteristics or other considerations (e.g., risk or extremely tight deadlines), less constructive styles may come into play.

For example, you may become a S3 negotiator and attempt to withdraw or hide behind policies or procedural issues and guidelines. Knowing our own individual style, based on input from testing, others, or actual practice negotiation sessions, may reveal that we tend to behave in an S3 fashion. However, when called upon we can meet the hard-driving demands of the S4 negotiator head on, or conversely try to smooth over the controversy by incorporating S2-like comments. Likewise, the other person with whom we are negotiating can significantly change his or her behavior during the course of a negotiation—often in response to our style.

Throughout this chapter we have tried to demonstrate the practical utilities of S1 behavior in virtually every situation. There is less to lose in behaving more collaborative with most other types of negotiators than there is by adapting a rigid S2, S3, or S4 style. In looking at the different interactions, clearly the impact of an S4 on both S2 and S3, can cause withdrawal (S3) or superficial agreement (S2) that represents very little real progress. S4-S4 negotiations usually result in many proposals being put forward but little understanding being achieved. Likewise, S2 behavior used with negotiators who prefer either S3 or S1 behavior, is likely to yield little in the way of real results. Often, little progress can be made with S3 because of the tendency to hide behind policies and procedures that may, in fact, be nonadaptive.

However, S2s (the accommodators) may be friendly to negotiate with but may not engender any real confidence or conviction that they are able to deliver once they have agreed to the terms of a negotiation. Their need to please and be accepted may far exceed their authority. This can quickly alienate and frustrate S1 and S4 negotiators, and create irreversible mistrust in S3 negotiators.

If during a negotiation session you sense a sudden shift from an S4 style to perhaps a S3 style, it should cause you to probe why such a change has occurred. If an S4 suddenly becomes S3, it's a good indication that he or she has perhaps lost interest and decided that the negotiation is not worth pursuing at this point. Conversely, if an S4 becomes an S2 it may be an indication that they have simply lost interest and are willing to placate you into believing that you have a relationship when in reality they are trying to end the discussion in a friendly fashion.

If a negotiation that starts out as an S1-S1 suddenly becomes an S4, there is good reason to stop and probe why the other person has reacted in such a way. It may be that time pressure has built up, a significant risk has been realized or some other relevant business or personal circumstance has come into the picture.

The trigger for this change may have nothing to do with the negotiation, and may be the result of other job-related pressures or personal circumstances. However, these other variables significantly affect the other person's negotiation style, and we must be extremely cautious with our reaction or overreaction to their sudden change.

While we have clearly indicated that S1 is the most important and productive negotiation style, there are circumstances when other styles of negotiating can seem to be more beneficial—but only in the short term.

CONCLUSION

We have discussed some of the pros and cons of each of the four negotiation styles: S1, S2, S3, and S4. The thrust of this book has been on establishing long-term relationships and on negotiating agreements that have significant impact on both individuals and/or their organizations. The following guidelines are intended to help individuals build long-term relationships in which negotiations may occur frequently over a period of time.

1. Be aware of your style and get in the practice of trying to estimate or anticipate the style of others with whom you will be negotiating.

2. Seek out feedback—honest, candid, specific—on your negotiating style.

3. During every negotiation interaction use the opportunity to try and further clarify the substantive issues and needs of the other party.

4. Try to listen to the underlying implications and the sometimes nonverbalized needs and agendas of others.

5. To every extent possible, maintain two-way conversations throughout the negotiation situation. Watch for periods of time when either you or the other party clearly seem to be dominating the conversation. If you notice this is the case, take action to break the rhythm, whether it be your own dominance or others.

6. Demonstrate understanding and attentiveness to the interests and needs of the other party. Use reflective statements, paraphrasing, and empathizing to demonstrate and confirm your understanding of their position. Ask questions about their statements to show interest and to clarify what they are really after.

7. Demonstrate your ability to be open-minded and accept reasonable, creative alternatives to the positions you came into the negotiation holding.

8. Work toward the creation of a problem-solving, problem-focused environment. Try to minimize emphasis on beginning positions and spend or invest time up front in clarifying the interests of both parties.

9. Try to minimize personality involvement and conflicts by focusing on the issues. If in fact you are dealing with a person you genuinely do not "like," extra effort must be given to keep the focus on substantive issues. You may never like or need to like the people you are working with or negotiating with, but you may be required to continue negotiations with them.

10. As appropriate, ask for advice regarding alternatives and creative solutions to the issues that you have posed. If suggestions on these issues are offered, recognize and reinforce these contributions and build on them whenever possible rather than attempting to initially discredit the suggestions.

11. Be willing to confront conflict and/or objections directly, but in a constructive fashion. Focus on the substance or impact of the conflict rather than the personality that may be causing it.

Notes

[1]An instrument designed to measure style tendencies is currently under development by the authors.

PART TWO

Deal Making:
The Process

We, the authors consider ourselves to be educators, believers in the principle, as Peter Drucker has put it, that people learn what they do. We are also believers in the inductive method. Chapters 6 through 10 seek to clarify and amplify the key concepts of negotiation by connecting them to pragmatic negotiation issues.

Through excerpts from interviews and fictionalized scenarios, the reader is coaxed to make the connections between the principles being discussed and their own and real-life applications of these principles.

CHAPTER 6

Transfer of Ownership: Buying and Selling a Business

A vice president of a major aerospace firm settled back on the couch, "There have been several problems that we never had to think about before. The main one is environmental." An expert at negotiating contracts for airplane engines, this V.P. was grappling with the problems associated with selling a subsidiary business. "When we took this site, environmental issues were much less important than they are now. However, we had a survey done to check for asbestos and that sort of thing . . . in fact, we gutted the building and rebuilt it. We were satisfied that it was a safe place for people to work. Now that we're selling it, most of the people who have looked at it or bid on it have immediately raised environmental issues as one of the first things: ground water pollution, chemical spills, asbestos, PCBs, and so forth."

"Nothing stays the same." While we're certain that this statement doesn't arrive as a big revelation to you, it is worth pondering for a moment as we begin our discussion on negotiating your way into or out of a business. There are two kinds of value associated with anything one would buy or sell: intrinsic value and extrinsic value. Intrinsic value relates to tangible items associated with what you are selling: inventory, fixtures, machinery, and so on. Extrinsic value refers to the intangibles, such as existing customer relationships, the expertise of your personnel, the positive recognition associated with your name, shifts in public attitudes toward products and by-products of your business such as pollution. Any transformation of ownership must begin with a consideration of the value, both intrinsic and extrinsic, of the business entity being transferred. This consideration will develop into the terms and conditions of the deal, and will supply all of the issues that must be negotiated.

WHY IS THE BUSINESS BEING SOLD?

It is not the purpose of this book to help you find a business to buy, or convince you to sell the one you have. We begin with the assumption that you have already made a decision to enter into a negotiation to either buy or sell and are in the planning stage. The first question you want to ask (from either side) is, *Why is this business for sale?*

In his book, *Buying and Selling a Business*, Robert F. Klueger says that often sellers are reluctant to tell prospective buyers the real reason they want to sell. It is always a good idea to remain suspicious and keep digging. Klueger lists three reasons why sellers sell businesses:

1. The seller isn't making enough money in the business
2. The seller has a personal reason for selling
3. The seller knows bad times are coming[1]

There are a few more that we would like to add:

4. The seller is reducing debt resulting from a leveraged buy out
5. The seller is committed to a particular business mix that doesn't include the company's products or services
6. The seller is the heir to a founder/owner who died

While most of the reasons are easy to detect and understand, the *personal* reasons for selling can be elusive. The owner may simply want to retire, or may be ill. The reason could also be a business divorce, where partners can no longer agree and refuse to sell out to each other. Klueger suggests that business divorces are much more common than might be expected.

In a negotiation, personal reasons are often advantageous for the buyer. If you are buying, spend some energy finding out if there may be personal reasons driving the deal. If so, they can mean a savings of money to you as well as more favorable terms and conditions. Ask around the industry, community, competition, and suppliers; the research may pay real dividends in information power.

The most dangerous situation facing a potential buyer is one in which the seller knows that business is going to get worse. At the time of this writing, there is a major subsidiary of a financial services company on the market that is very profitable and attractive. However, a careful look at financial statements from the last few years will reveal a startling drop in profitability. In addition, the company had based its future growth on a product that has failed, while similar products that should be successful are about to hit the market.

The potential pitfalls on the buying side of a transfer of ownership help us to highlight the focus point of this chapter: *focus on planning the deal*. Do your homework! Ask yourself, the seller, and others who may have pertinent information questions like the following.

1. What has been the financial history of this business in the last five years?

2. What changes in management immediately precede or coincide with the sale?

3. What technology or processes is the business dependent upon for profitability?

4. What support is necessary from outside the company, for example, materials, software, distribution?

5. How will a transfer of ownership affect key personnel? Customers?

6. What is the competition doing?

7. Does the company have a strategic plan? If so, how is it working?

8. What is happening in the employment marketplace? Is personnel becoming harder to find? Are wages going up?

9. What are lease commitments, expiration dates?
10. What loans are outstanding? Due?
11. How will a transfer in ownership affect existing contracts?
12. Is the company involved in any litigation?

While these questions do not represent a comprehensive list, they should cue the potential buyer to some of the areas of possible problems. In addition, the seller also needs to ask questions like this in preparation for the negotiation. Since these questions will probably be asked, you should have answers ready. Vague or evasive answers to issues perceived as critical aspects of a deal will erode trust and make agreement more difficult.

"How big a deal was this?" We asked.

The V.P. reflected. "It was . . . umm, the cash that would have changed hands would have been $6 million. But, it was bigger than that in that we were being paid $6 million, and they were also assuming some liabilities that we had. I don't know how they valued those liabilities. We valued them at another $5 or $6 million. They may have valued them completely differently. They were taking over some leases that we had and our order backlog, which we particularly wanted to make sure was completed. They were taking over the employees, because one of our objectives was to try and protect the employees to the best of our ability. One option has always been to close down. That's still our option if this deal doesn't work. . . ."

WHAT IS IMPORTANT TO THE OTHER NEGOTIATOR?

The excerpt just discussed brings home the point that parties on opposite sides of a negotiation tend to value parts of the deal differently. In his planning, the V.P. had set a value range for the leases and order backlog. However, he was also committed to protecting the employees. On the other side, those employees also have extrinsic value. The business being sold is highly technical in nature, and it is safe to assume that much of the staff is made up of highly skilled labor that would be difficult to replace. These are all factors that influence the total value of a deal. There are several formulas for valuing a business based on analyses of financial statements. These provide excellent benchmarks for setting the ranges of your potential deal. But, despite what the formulas tell you, a business is worth what a buyer will pay and a seller will take.

THE PRENEGOTIATION PLAN

Our focus in this chapter is on planning, and it is axiomatic to say that planning is an important part of the negotiation process. Like other endeavors both in and outside of the business world, planning is a key element of success. There are so many things that you can't control during a negotiation that getting a firm grasp of the things you can control is very meaningful. You cannot be overprepared for a negotiation, you can only be underprepared. Preparation can be the major source of your power during the negotiation.

While every negotiation has its own special preparation requirements, the following questions prompt a wide range of preparatory activities to be considered before sitting down at the table.

When Is the Negotiation Taking Place?

The buyer in a transfer of ownership negotiation generally has more control over timing than the seller. It can be useful for the buyer to discover fluctuations in the business cycle, impending demands on cash flow, or any other factors influencing the urgency of the sale.

How Much Time Do You Have to Reach a Conclusion?

All other things being equal, progress in a negotiation will accelerate when one or both parties approach a deadline. In selling the subsidiary, the V.P. was continually facing the prospect that the parent company would tire of the process and simply shut the facility down.

What Are the Issues to Be Negotiated?

The more experienced a negotiator is, the more issues he or she sees to be negotiated. A negotiable issue is anything that has (or may have) value to either the buyer or seller. The buyer in our example may not be as concerned about retaining the labor force as is the seller. However, knowing this is important to the seller gives this issue value as a tradeoff for something else, such as a lower price.

What Are the Issues to Be Avoided?

It is foolish to think that any of the major issues in a negotiation will not be raised. Regardless of the strength or weakness of your position, you must be prepared to answer questions on these issues. In our example, the environmental issue ultimately outweighed price and all other issues, and a failure to resolve it killed the deal. Any issue, large or small, that you are not prepared to discuss will likely be decided in the other side's favor. Having said that, we need to qualify our point by adding that you never offer up anything that you are sure to lose. Never start a discussion on any issue on which you have a weak position.

How Should the Issues Be Prioritized?

Once you have created your list of issues, you have to rate them in terms of their relative importance. Use a three-part scheme for rating an issue: the top level is "need to have," second level is "nice to have," and a third level is "tradeoff." Need to have is an issue that you must win. Without it, there's no deal. If you don't get what you want or need, you will walk away from the table. A nice to have is an issue that is very desirable for you. An issue that you will go to great lengths to have decided in your favor. A tradeoff is an issue that is readily available for tradeoff; all issues that are neither musts nor wants. The more tradeoffs you have, the more flexibility you have during a negotiation.

How Is Each Issue Valued?

We began the chapter with a discussion of intrinsic and extrinsic value. It would appear that it is easier to pin a dollar value on an intrinsic item, such as a building or a machine, than on an extrinsic item, such as the closing date or the value of a trained and productive staff. However, with a little thought and effort, you can place a monetary value on every issue you have listed. It is very important to consider what the value of a particular issue is to the other negotiator.

Often you will find that issues which are of no great consequence to you have a high value to the other side. The inexperienced negotiator tends to throw these in, rather than using them as powerful bargaining points.

Do We Negotiate as a Team or Individually?

Negotiating with a team enhances your resources and, very often, you need others to help in the decision-making or information review process. If there are legal issues, you probably want a lawyer present. If there are complex monetary issues, you probably want an accountant present. However, it should always be clear that there is one person designated as the leader for your team.

What Are Your Authority Limits?

You cannot negotiate effectively without knowing the limits of your authority to make a deal. If you are the principal in a deal, then there shouldn't be a problem unless you have stockholders to answer to. Most negotiations do not take place between principals. We often find ourselves negotiating for our companies without absolute authority. On the whole, you want to enter a negotiation with the highest level of authority possible. This gives you confidence, makes your presentation stronger, and develops the other side's sense of respect for you. It is not a good practice to admit that you have absolute authority, since you may want to have a reason to review new offers or issues with "others." If you have claimed ultimate authority, you may be pressed for an immediate decision, having minimized your avenues of temporary escape.

What Are the Facts?

This step is all encompassing. The more you know about a deal and the other side, the more effective you will be in a negotiation. As we said before, *you cannot be overprepared for a negotiation, only underprepared.* It is not enough to know about the balance sheet of a business, if you don't know that there are expensive environmental problems waiting in the wings.

There is always a tendency to want a deal to work out. Or, to put it another way, most people do not initiate the buying or selling of a business with the idea in mind that it won't work out. Therefore, there is pressure to see the deal in a positive light, or worse, to see things in the deal that aren't there. In the mind of a motivated buyer or seller, a vaguely supported assumption can seem like a solid fact.

The following list of factors is supplied by the IRS as criteria for valuing a business.

1. The nature and history of the business.
2. The economic outlook in general and the specific industry in particular.
3. Book value, financial condition, and earning capacity.
4. Dividend-paying capacity.
5. Does the business have some intangible value?
6. Prior sales of the company's stock.
7. Market price of similar businesses.

During any negotiation, the rule of thumb is that the person who is asking the most questions is doing better than the person who provides most of the answers. The questioner has two advantages: (1) maintains control of the communication, and (2) acquires more of the necessary information. Take some time during your preparation to write down a list of questions to ask during the negotiation. In this way you will always have a relevant question ready when the opportunity presents itself.

What Is the Other Side's Point of View?

Again, the key here for negotiation purposes is what the other side values, and how the other side values your potential give points. Not knowing this makes you susceptible to a phony issue tactic; where the other side emphasizes an issue that is not their major target in order to get you to concede what they want if they back away from the one they seem so tenacious about.

Spend a great deal of preparatory time trying to see the deal through the other negotiator's eyes. *Pretend that you are entering a debate and must learn both sides of an issue and be prepared to defend either side if called on to do so.* How does the other side view you? What does the other side think is important to you? Are they right? What will be the main issues they will raise? How badly do they need this deal? Who is advising them? Who can walk away with the least risk? Why?

What Do I Know About the Other Negotiator(s)?

We have demonstrated continually in our workshops that given the same parameters, different negotiating teams or individuals will achieve widely divergent results. The factors that surround real negotiations as opposed to the workshop role playing will tend to minimize these differences but not eradicate them. We believe in the principle of *different people, different outcome.* What are the other negotiator's attitudes, values, beliefs, and prejudices? What is his or her style? How do these characteristics differ from mine? How do these factors influence me? What do I know (or what can I find out) about how effective the other person is as a negotiator?

What Outside Influences May Affect the Negotiation?

Very often, as in our opening example, there are outside influences that affect the conduct and outcome of a negotiation. The following checklist can be used as a guide to many of the potential outside influences that can affect a negotiation.

1. Current market conditions
2. Laws and regulations
3. Government action
4. Action by your competitors
5. Any materials or supplies in short supply
6. The inflation rate
7. An action or possible action by a foreign nation
8. The stock market
9. An upcoming political election
10. An upcoming union election
11. Any personal problems

What Are Your Acceptable Ranges for the Deal?

Some of your most important planning centers around your complete understanding of the ranges of acceptability for all of the issues contained in the potential deal. Based on your understanding (or speculation) about the prospect's needs, lay out the components of your *best possible deal.* Use Figure 6.1 of the negotiation process as a guideline for your thinking.

Figure 6.1. Negotiation Process: Acceptable and Nonacceptable Deal Ranges

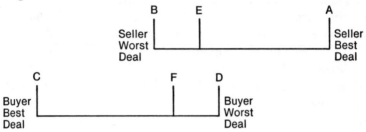

In Figure 6.1, assume you are the seller.

Your best possible deal is at point A.

Point B is your least acceptable deal—the level below which you cannot go.

Point C is the best possible deal from the buyer's point of view.

Point D is the point beyond which the buyer cannot accept the deal.

The limits of any agreement will fall between point B and point D; since the buyer will not buy above D, and you cannot sell below B, any agreement between buyer and seller must be somewhere between points B and D. The probable case scenario in a negotiation between two experienced negotiators of equal skill will result in a deal somewhere between points E and F. Skill levels can significantly affect where the deal settles. In setting the ranges of your acceptable deal, remember that you will never get more than you ask for, or pay less than you initially offer.

In the type of deal that has many components, such as buying or selling a business, all of the major factors should be diagrammed this way, since there is bound to be more than one deal breaker in the list of issues to be negotiated. The skilled negotiator remains continually aware of the relationship between the issues and how the give and take of negotiation affects the overall deal range.

Figure 6.2 is one way of graphically representing the relative values of various deal components. By listing each component of a deal and considering where these components must fall in relation to one another, you can maintain better control during the negotiation. In Chapter 7, we discuss the *rheostat principle*, which details this approach more fully.

What Is Your Plan of Action?

If you can seize the initiative and set some of the rules for the negotiation procedure, you are in a better position to influence the outcome. Develop an ideal agenda. What would you like to discuss

Figure 6.2. Deal Chart
Deal Components

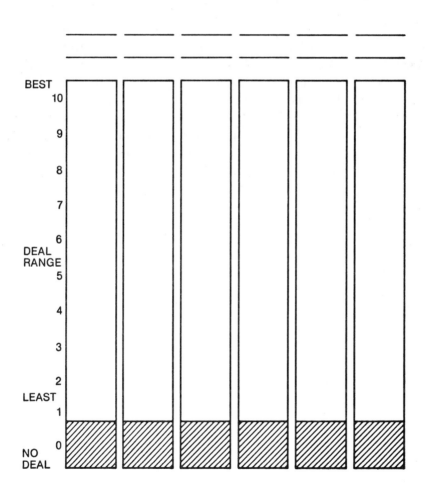

first? Second? Last? Settling on an agenda will probably be your first actual negotiation issue. In problem-solving negotiation, you want to avoid the quick settlement of supposedly minor issues at the outset, since the relative importance and value of issues can shift considerably during the course of negotiation. Be sensitive to the fact that more concessions are generally made late in the negotiation process, often because the people just want to end it! Don't make many concessions up front, and end up out of ammunition near the deadline. The issues that will receive the most attention are those that occur at the beginning when everyone is fresh and wants to put on a good show.

Have You Used Role Play to Practice Your Approach?

It has been said that if there is one thing that should never surprise you, it's the sound of your own voice. There is no substitute for practice. You need to seek out someone, perhaps on your team, who will take on the role of the other side. This gives you the opportunity to ask and field questions in a simulated environment. Thinking through your approach in quiet solitude may help arrange your thoughts and provide some insights, but it is not an effective rehearsal. In addition, your partner in the rehearsal can provide you with perceptions that you would ordinarily not have access to, (e.g., mannerisms that may be signaling insecurity or anxiousness). If your role play partner is familiar with the deal, much can be gained by having that person take on the role you will assume during the actual negotiation, allowing you to play the other side. This approach will greatly enhance your empathy and perspective of the other side's position. It also shows where there are holes in your preparation or arguments.

NEGOTIATION PLANNING FORM

Many of the points discussed have been incorporated in Figure 6.3, Negotiation Planning Form, which appears at the end of the chapter. Each main section of the form will now be discussed.

Objectives and Strategy

Objectives. The first consideration in your planning process is to work through your objectives.

What do I want to accomplish overall?

What do I want to accomplish with the first stage of the negotiation? The second? The third?

What are my business objectives? My personal objectives?

A clear understanding of *your objectives* at the outset of planning provides the reference points that keep you on track as you go through the process. Everything you plan and execute should be evaluated against these objectives.

Situational Factors. Another area of examination is situational factors. Situational factors refer to the means through which you became involved in this negotiation in the first place, and any special circumstances about the situation or the other person that either enhance or impede your negotiating position.

Have you negotiated with this person before?

Why has this person agreed to negotiate with you?

Other Negotiator's Primary Needs

Some of your most important planning centers around your anticipation of what the other negotiator's thinking. Try to put yourself in the other negotiator's place; what do you perceive as the other person's primary needs?

Also, ask yourself, if you were this person, how would you rank these needs in order of importance? Very often, by the time you get down to serious negotiation, you have a clear idea of what the needs are. An understanding of the other person's needs is the basis for your strategic planning.

Based on your understanding (or speculation) about the other person's needs, lay out the components of your best possible deal.

As part of your planning, make a list of all the negotiation materials you may need. Bring notes from previous calls, and proposals or letters that have been exchanged, or sample materials you intend to use for proof.

Consider the Environment

Environment plays an important part in negotiation. Questions to ask yourself should include:

Figure 6.3. Negotiation Planning Form

Objectives and Strategy

A. What Are Your Objectives (short term, long term, business, personal)?

_____

_____

_____

_____

B. What Situational Factors May Influence the Outcome?

_____

_____

_____

_____

C. What Are the Other Negotiator's Objectives (business, personal)?

_____

_____

_____

_____

D. What Are the Other Negotiator's Needs? (As you understand them at this this stage)

_____

_____

_____

_____

E. What is Your Best Possible Deal?

_____

_____

_____

_____

F. What is Your Least Acceptable Deal?

_____

_____

_____

_____

_____

Negotiation Materials

A. Notes? Records? _____

   Documents? _____

   Proposals? _____

   Audiovisual? _____

B. Other Materials:

_____

_____

_____

_____

_____

Environment

A. When Should Meeting Take Place? _____

Where? _____

Who Should Be There? _____
B. Other Considerations:

_____

_____

_____

_____

_____

Outline General Approach

A. How Will You Begin?

_____

_____

_____

_____

_____

B. Key Questions to Ask:

_____

_____

_____

_____

_____

C. Alternative Acceptable Combinations (if/then):

_____

_____

_____

_____

_____

Where will the meeting take place? What building? What room?
Will others be present? Who? Why?
What will you wear?

Outline Your General Approach

Now that you have examined or speculated on the needs of both sides
and considered the positions, you should develop a script of how you
would like to see the negotiation proceed, an outline of your general
approach. Picture yourself in the negotiation.

What will happen first? What will you say?

What is a good opening line to move from rapport to business?

Make a list of key questions that you can refer to at appropriate
moments during the negotiation.

CONCLUSION

Because you are dealing with situations that have many components, it is essential that you examine the various combinations of any
potential deal very carefully.

As stated earlier, you cannot overprepare for a negotiation—only
underprepare. The planning for what follows highlights many of the
areas you should consider in your prenegotiation planning. However,
you must consider and add unique variables related to your particular
negotiation situation.

Notes

[1] Robert F. Klueger, *Buying and Selling a Business: A Step-by-Step Guide* (New York: Wiley), p. 10.

CHAPTER 7

Negotiating Leases and Acquisitions

When we arrived at the restaurant to meet with a high level executive of a major advertising firm, it was not yet the bustling, somewhat noisy place it would become in a short while. While waiting for our luncheon partner, we recalled this man's successful climb to the top. A CPA educated in local New York City schools, the executive brought neither connections nor a particular genius for numbers to his profession. What's the secret of his success? He negotiates great deals. The secret to his dealmaking? He pays attention to detail.

When he arrives, he doffs his hat, which has a brim that's a bit too wide for an accountant—but appropriate for a major advertising executive. We can see even at the distance between the table and the coat room that he is excited. After some niceties and brief exchanges of information about our families, general health, and so forth, I ask, "So, how's the lease deal going?" I knew immediately that I had struck the right nerve. He was currently engaged in negotiating for new office space for the company. His eyes narrowed, I thought I could see his ears slick back against his head. He leaned forward. "I got them to throw in the paper towels and the toilet paper," he confided in triumph. He settled back in his chair comfortably, awaiting my admiration to wash over him. I stammered, "The toilet paper . . . ?"

We are given one of those looks reserved for children who just don't get it, and then he proceeded to whip out his pen. He began firing questions at me, and without waiting for answers scribbled notes furiously on the tablecloth. "How many people including visitors will be in the offices during any given day? Week? Month?" "How many times will they use the bathroom?" "How many sheets of tissue will the average person use on each visit?" "How many sheets on a roll?" "How many rolls per week? Month? Year?" "What is the cost per roll?" "How many towels?" "Cost . . . ?" He finished with a flourish that bisected the table-cloth from end to end with ballpoint precision and boomed, "It's worth a hundred thousand dollars!"

THE ROLE OF THE CONTRACT

Taking initiative and attending to details are important factors in negotiation regardless of the items or issues under consideration. However, nowhere is this more evident than in deals involving the acquisition or leasing of real estate. Such transactions invariably involve lengthy and precisely worded contracts. We are not experts in contract law, and that is not the focus of this book. However, the activities that take place between parties before and during the contract writing process are fertile ground for negotiation practices. A real estate purchase or leasing contract is a legally binding agreement in which the parties describe the terms of the deal, define the property being sold or leased, and allocate between buyer and seller or lessor and lessee the various risks that are inherent in the transaction. Skillful dealmakers view the contract as a dynamic and creative process that turns a verbal understanding into a written agreement. In the words of Dennis H. Horn, in a passage taken from his book, *Negotiating Real Estate Transactions*:

A well written contract protects all parties. In the negotiating and drafting process, the parties are forced to confront and find solutions for a series of potential problems. . . . Ambiguous contracts lead to frustration and sometimes litigation. Although both buyer and seller benefit from a thorough contract, the negotiating process itself is like a chess game where one side or the other can gain significant advantage through preparation and tactical skill.[1]

Although we focus more on the specifics of planning in Chapter 8, it should be obvious that knowing what you want and being able to address the other person's concerns can provide you with a competitive advantage. As our advertising executive pointed out, owners tend to be tough and tactical. Their tendency is to try to push their costs onto you.

Price is always the kingpin of a real estate transaction. However, other factors (e.g., the closing date, financing, and a variety of other economic considerations) can have a strong influence on the acceptability of any deal. The two parties involved will have different goals and objectives for a successful outcome. The owner wants a good price and a firm date—preferably as soon as possible. The owner also wants to eliminate any contingent liability. In a buy/sell situation, the seller will want to eliminate conditions of the closing that are out of control. Horn gives us an example: "if there is a fire or other casualty before closing, the seller would like the buyer to be forced to close and accept assignment of the insurance proceeds."[2]

The ideal lessor's or seller's contract contains the following provisions:

1. A clear identification of the parties in the deal
2. A clear description of the property being sold or leased
3. A statement of the economic terms including the deposit, the price, the closing or signing date, and any other monetary arrangements
4. A statement that the property is sold or leased "as is"
5. A statement that at closing or signing the buyer or lessee assumes all risks with respect to the property

Of course, price is equally important to the buyer or lessee; however, there are other concerns. Our vice chairman puts it this way: "What do I want done that I don't want to pay for?" A buyer must be very detailed about assigning the risks, since the doctrine of caveat emptor still prevails in commercial real estate transactions. That is, a buyer may be assuming risks that have not been specifically allocated in a contract.

The ideal lessee's or buyer's contract contains the following provisions:

1. A clear statement that the property is tied up
2. A complete and accurate description of the property
3. A clear understanding that all preclosing conditions (e.g., a good title, zoning restrictions, and environmental issues) have been met
4. The reversion of all risks to the seller or lessor, including changes in the property before closing or signing
5. A statement of obligation on the part of the seller or lessor to assume any risks or repair any defects in the property that appear or become evident after closing or signing.

It is the conflict that arises out of the clash between opposing objectives that provides the opportunity and necessity for negotiation.

Contracts can be very complicated documents. They try to cover issues that potentially create problems for the parties involved. Some of these issues are nonnegotiable, such as the need for both parties to have the legal capacity to act. Most of the negotiation takes place around the terms of the agreement. Terms include the price, closing date, method of payment, distribution of existing fixtures, and the costs and liabilities assigned to each party.

THE ROLE OF THE ATTORNEY

Because of the complexity of these agreements and the large sums of money involved, most parties in a lease or purchase agreement retain attorneys. These third parties become an integral part of the negotiation process, and they often play the primary role of negotiating the deal. The attorney's role in this transaction is to point out the risks and opportunities of the deal as he sees them, and to provide technical assistance in the formulation of the language of the contract.

This relationship between client and attorney gives rise to tactical considerations during the negotiation process. Dennis Horn actually advocates the use of the "good guy/bad guy" tactic. "One successful negotiating strategy is for one person to play the good guy and the other to play the bad guy. The bad guy asks the hard questions and takes aggressive stances in the negotiation. The good guy steps in to pour oil on the waters and reach an agreement."[3]

However, he tempers his view on the value of tactics with the following caution:

> No deal will be consummated unless there is a certain amount of give and take between the buyer and seller. The negotiator who takes a hard-line position on every point risks losing the deal. On the other hand, you rarely win a point in negotiation unless you make the request.[4]

While we don't advocate a tactical approach, anyone entering a real estate negotiation is well advised to watch for the use of tactics and take the appropriate countermeasures. We certainly agree with Horn that effective negotiation requires that you put all of the issues on the table. We have said it before: one of the most frequent failures in negotiation is the failure to perceive issues that can be negotiated.

The attorney/client relationship is at once essential and problematic in negotiation. Sometimes the attorney takes too large a role and actually makes business decisions for the client. As a client in this situation, keep in mind who is really taking the risk. We can remember a particular tax audit we once went through that illustrates this point. Our accountant was there, and he rose to the occasion. He argued all the points, presented all the evidence while, we, the clients, sat on the sidelines, detached, and entertained by the "theater" of the experience. We were startled at the end when he turned to us and said, "Okay, write a check for $500." I was immediately reminded whose audit this was.

PROMOTING MUTUAL INVESTMENT

Once initiated, deals take on lives of their own. They begin as embryos and progress through several stages of development. Along the way they can experience retrogression or sudden spurts of growth and change. Ultimately, they either happen or sicken and die. As with its organic counterpart, the birth of a deal requires two parties with mutually dependent goals. Regardless of which side of the deal you are on, you don't want to be in the position of having expended large or disproportionate amounts of time, energy, resources, and dollars trying to make a deal happen when the other side has invested little and ultimately walks away.

In his book called *Dealmaker*, Robert Lawrence Kuhn talks about his friend and business associate, Charles Hurwitz, CEO of MCO Holdings in Houston. Kuhn calls Hurwitz a "Superb Dealmaker." He says:

> [he] has a basic principle for developing large real estate properties with potential partners. He insists that the top executive of the possible joint venture see the property personally before beginning serious negotiations. Sure, the lieutenants have to go first. Sure the numbers have to work. But Hurwitz won't start the deal-making process until number one on the other side has actually trod the earth. "I want to see personal commitment, even enthusiasm," Hurwitz says. "I don't want to be three months down the road and then suddenly he finds something better to do. I also want to eliminate the excuse of 'well, you know I never actually saw the site.' "[5]

Ultimately, you cannot control the level of interest on the other side. However, here are some ways that mutual interest can be promoted.

1. Never let on that the party you are negotiating with is the only one currently in play. The less said about other potential players the better. If you lie about other opportunities, the verity of your statements can usually be checked. Even if there are other interested parties, you are under no obligation to name them, and should not.

2. If you are a seller or lessor trying to unload a property, don't sell too hard. Let the other side drift into the deal and sell themselves. You want them to invest time and money in evaluating the deal. A prospect is less likely to walk away if he or she has to justify the loss of an investment already made.

3. Deal directly with the owner's broker because the owner's broker doesn't have to split commission. This is strong incentive, and can be used for leverage in your favor.

BALANCING DEAL COMPONENTS

In an earlier chapter, we discussed the concept of value and how a single negotiating point can have a different degree of importance to each side of the negotiation, which is integral in determining the factor's importance to the outcome. In large transactions—such as real estate deals—the tendency is to focus on the numbers simply because the numbers are large. The purchase price or square foot price is also a variable that can be measured against the marketplace to determine if the numbers are realistic. Every deal has other components that represent relative value to the parties involved in the negotiation. In the same way our executive was able to turn paper towels and toilet paper into a meaningful saving on costs, close attention to the details of the transaction can yield benefits and, even more important, can provide alternative ways of balancing a deal so that everyone walks away with what is needed.

In a real estate transaction, factors such as location, size, configuration, and price are obvious value issues. The following is a list of other potential factors that could have significant value to one or both of the negotiating parties.

Date of closing

Date of occupancy

Allocation of responsibility and risk

Potential delay

Method of payment

Financing

Tax considerations

Term

Option to extend

Agent commission

Deferred fee agreement

Option to expand

Cost of living rent adjustment

Tax and common expense escalation

Restrictions on use

Maintenance and repairs

Alterations

Insurance liability

Assignment and subletting

Parking availability

Existing fixtures and equipment

Surveys

Environmental reports

Previously negotiated service contracts and agreements

Developing a sensitivity to the detailed value components of a deal is important in two ways. First, it promotes creative problem solving at points where conflict threatens to scuttle a deal. Simply having some valuable alternatives to either seek or give away keeps the parties talking and fuels the negotiation process. Second, by understanding which components are of value to you and which are not, you can maintain a profitable balance as each component is being negotiated. This approach is what we call the *rheostat principle*. Consider the following example.

Let's say you are negotiating for leased space in an office building. Certainly price is important, but you are also concerned about alterations, electric service, trunk lines for your phones and computers, and the term of the lease. The average rate for space in your category is $19 per square foot; you want to pay $18. The landlord is asking for $21. Your flexibility on the rent issue is dependent upon concessions on the other factors.

Ask the question, "How much would it cost me to make the necessary alterations? Run the wire, and so on?" Your leverage for lowering the rent is tied up in the same factors, and perhaps in some others that are of higher value to the landlord than they are to you (e.g., insurance liability or the existing fixtures and equipment).

In the rheostat principle, all of the special issues of a deal should be clustered under the broadest headings (what we call components) that make sense. For example, most deals—not just real estate transactions—have components that will fit under the following headings: Finance, Service, Liability/Risk, Assets, Timing, and Relationship. (See Figure 7.1.) Your particular negotiation situation may have more or fewer components, and perhaps some unique components. For

Figure 7.1. Deal Chart: Components
Deal Issues

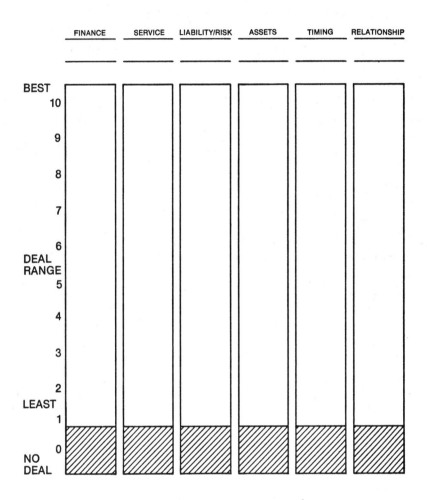

explanation purposes, let's look at these components with regard to our real estate deal.

Finance covers all of the costs associated with a deal: the rent, the purchase price, the cost of changes or renovations, financing costs, and any other dollar amounts associated with the cost of doing the deal.

Service includes all of the components associated with ongoing commitments: maintenance, repairs, account servicing, management reports, and so forth.

Liability/Risk are the costs or potential costs connected with insurance, liabilities, environmental concerns, or any other items or circumstances that could pose a legal or financial problem.

Assets refers to the existing assets of the deal where appropriate. Such things as building fixtures, equipment, cash on hand, and receivables fall into this category.

Timing can play a significant role in a negotiation. You need to consider what would be the relative value of consummating the deal sooner, later, or by a specific deadline. This could be determined by the expiration date of a current lease, by the end of a tax period, and many other factors.

Relationship can carry exceptional weight in the outcome of a deal, and can be ascribed a value based on the need for the parties to continue to do business with one another.

Each component is made up of numerous specific issues (See Figure 7.2). For example, the Financial component may include issues such as rent, cost of wiring, alteration expenses, broker's fees, and attorney's charges.

As shown in Figure 7.2, which graphically demonstrates the rheostat principle for our hypothetical lease deal, each of the issues listed under a component can be ascribed a value. "What is it worth to me to have the other party pick up the cost of maintenance, insurance, and so on." As part of your planning process, determine what your best possible deal would be for each item. Then, calculate how adjustments within the columns would balance one another. For example, if the landlord would be willing to pick up the cost of alterations, would you be willing to pay more rent? If so, how much? Set up subcharts of these column values as in Figure 7.2.

Perhaps the landlord has a cash-flow problem and would be willing to lower the rent if you took on some of the cost of the alterations. Maybe your specifications for wiring are so sensitive that you would rather maintain control of the contracting anyway. Are there any tax advantages for one party or the other in the assumption of some costs?

Next, look at how adjustments in one column would balance adjustments in the other columns. The result should approximate the effect you get when you adjust the lighting in a room controlled by several rheostats. By raising and lowering the various levers, you can maintain in the same overall light level, but with different accents and shading. When some of the levers are too low, the room is too dark. In the same way, when some of the components of the deal are at

Figure 7.2. Deal Chart: Finance Issue Components

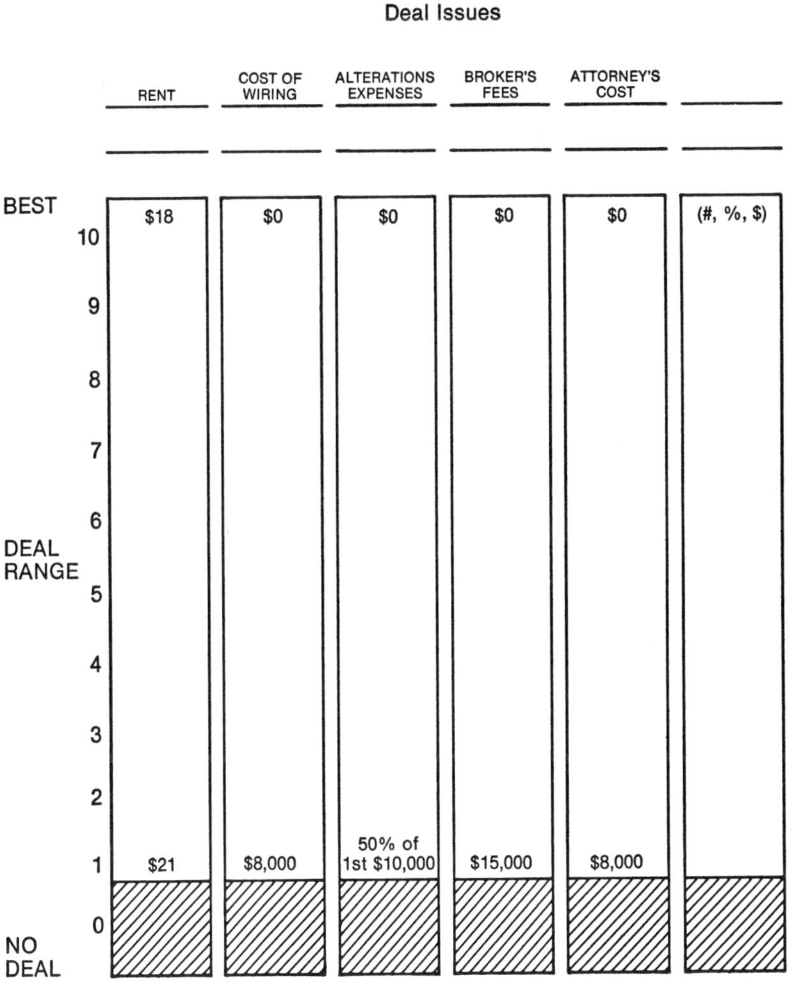

Deal Issues

	RENT	COST OF WIRING	ALTERATIONS EXPENSES	BROKER'S FEES	ATTORNEY'S COST	
BEST 10	$18	$0	$0	$0	$0	(#, %, $)
9						
8						
7						
6						
DEAL RANGE 5						
4						
3						
2						
1	$21	$8,000	50% of 1st $10,000	$15,000	$8,000	
NO DEAL 0						

unacceptable value levels, you stand to be a loser. The key is to be aware of these components and be sensitive to the relationship that exists among them. It is the attention to this kind of detail that will make you a better negotiator.

In Chapter 6 we discussed the determination of acceptable deal ranges as an important part of the planning process. We introduced the model seen in Figure 7.3 (repeat of Figure 6.1).

The limits of any acceptable deal will fall between point B and Point D. This holds true for lessor and lessee as well as buyer and

Figure 7.3.   Negotiation Process: Acceptable and Nonacceptable Deal Ranges

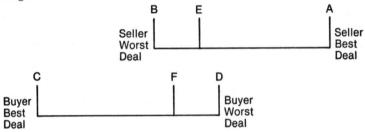

seller. As we said before, the probable case scenario in a negotiation between two experienced negotiators of equal skill will result in a deal somewhere between points E and F. Because this is such a narrow range, in most cases your attention to the details of the deal's components can spell the difference between a good or a bad deal for you.

INITIATING THE DEAL

If you are buying a house, you generally make an offer to the owner either directly or through the owner's broker. This offer can be written or verbal, and depending on the accepted practice in your area, may be accompanied by a check for up to 1 percent of the offering price to "bind" the deal. After the offer is accepted, its validity is usually contingent on several factors. These include: acceptable financing, favorable inspection by a qualified engineer, the inclusion or removal of certain fixtures or other tangibles associated with the subject property, and a mutually convenient closing date. If the offer is acceptable to the owner, a contract is drawn up which reflects the understanding between the two parties and covers all of the legalities peculiar to your locality.

If the bid is not acceptable in its original form, the owner makes a counteroffer. Because of the interposition of the broker (often more than one), the principals involved in such a deal rarely sit down and negotiate. The situation might change considerably if you are dealing directly with the owner. An owner can sell the same property for less if a broker's commission isn't involved. This requires you to seek out and initiate purchases and leases directly with owners. As part of this process, you will be committing time and resources that need to be valued against the potential effect of a broker's fees.

Relationship values also come into play. You may like each other, or, more importantly, the owner may feel comfortable about passing the old homestead into the hands of such a fine and upstanding person as yourself and be willing to take less money. However, the owner may find you repugnant and decide not to sell to you at any price. (Recall the scenario described in Chapter 5, "The Great House Purchase Saga.")

Brokers are often valuable and worthy intermediaries—they are paid well for their services. Remember, if you are the buyer, that same broker who has been ushering you around, buying you lunch, and now seems like an old friend with your best interests at heart, works for the seller. And, the size of this broker's commission depends directly on how much you pay for the property.

The best advice is to remember that whether you are talking to the owner or to an intermediary, you are negotiating. You must be careful about the amount and kind of information you provide. Ultimately, no one but you should be aware of your bottom-line figure.

When it comes to leasing commercial space, many of the same principles hold true. While some proportion of these transactions still involve the owner directly, most major deals are done through a broker. The deal is initiated through discussion with the broker on terms and conditions, and formalized with a written proposal. The proposal should be as detailed as is practical, and should represent the level at which you are prepared to close a deal. Typical categories covered in a proposal letter include:

Rent (per square foot for each year of lease)

Rental space (square foot gross)

Escalation (tax or cost of living)

Electric (who pays, and how it is billed)

Term (length of lease plus options)

Concession (on rent)

Availability

Options (on additional space)

Security (equipment and personnel)

Freight elevator (time restrictions?)

Work by landlord (renovation, alterations, code adherence in rental space)

Building repairs (lobby, elevators, lighting, etc.)

Restrictions (removal of other current tenants, restrictions on future tenants who move in)

The owner then responds in writing, indicating what items are acceptable as is, and what modifications are necessary on items which are unacceptable as proposed. The following two letters were taken from an actual deal that was initiated and completed. The names of the companies have been changed. These are offered as examples, not necessarily models to follow precisely.

September 6, 1989

Mr. John Smith
Senior Vice President
Acme Real Estate Company
650 Madison Avenue
New York, NY 10017

RE: 21 East 20th Street

Dear John:

ABC Communications, Inc. hereby offers to rent the 11th and 12th floors of the above property.

Rent:	$11 per square foot first five years., $12 per square foot next five years.
Rental Space:	11500 square foot per floor gross.
Escalation:	1 cent per 1 cent. Base year: 1990.
Electric:	Direct meter, power to be minimum of 450 amps per floor.
Term:	Ten years with option to renew.

Name of Building:	To be ABC Communications, Inc.
Concession:	Three months construction time. Six months free rent.
Availability:	January 1, 1990 to begin construction.
Options:	Tenth floor to coincide with expiration of above term at the lower of market or rental in effect at time of excise option.
Security:	Full-time security from 7:30 a.m.–8:00 p.m., five days per week in addition to a security system for after hours entrance. Seven days access with key.
Freight Elevator:	Available for mail room and messenger use, no time restrictions.

Work by Landlord:	1. New windows all around.
	2. New elevator doors on floors including freight doors.
	3. New fire exit doors with alarm.
	4. New bathrooms to consist of: two per floor
	  – two men's (two commodes, two urinals per room)
	  – two women's (three commodes per room).
	5. Repair weak spots on wood floors.
	6. Reasonable garbage removal rates.

Building Repairs:	1. Passenger elevator refurbished, tenant has right of approval. 2. Lobby refurbished, tenant has right of approval. Includes lighting doors and security desk.
Restrictions:	Removal of copy shop from building and rental of commercial store front space to prime "A" tenant.

We are looking forward to hearing from you at your earliest convenience.

Cordially,

Janice Jones

Negotiation on various points ensued, and the following summary of understanding was sent to the prospect by the broker.

Real Estate Location
21 East 20th Street
New York, N.Y.

	ABC's Offering Letter	Landlord Response
Space	Floors 11 and 12 at 11,500 per square foot gross.	Accepts.
Rent: Ten Year Lease	$11 1st five years. $12 next five years.	Accepts.
Escalation	1 cent per 1 cent. Base year 1990.	Accepts.
Electric	Direct meter	Accepts.
Term	Ten years with option to renew.	Accepts.
Name on Building	ABC Communications, Inc.	Accepts.
Concession	Three months construction. Six months free rent and construction of new windows, bathrooms, elevator doors, fire exit doors, and freight doors.	1. Twelve months free rent. ABC is to assume new construction (windows, bathrooms, etc.). 2. Three months free rent and provide construction elevator door.
Availability	January 1, 1990	Available in January 1990
Options	Tenth floor to coincide with above	No floors currently available
Security	Full-time concierge from 7:30 a.m.–8:00 p.m. five days in addition to after hours security.	Install concierge desk and supply guard from 8 a.m.–6 p.m. and after hours security system.
Freight Elevator	Use by messenger/mail people.	Agree. Available only during work hours.

| Building Repair | Refurbish elevator and lobby, tenants have right of approval. | Landlord will improve lighting in passenger lobby and replace entrance doors. |

As you can see by comparing the offering letter with the summary of terms, there was considerable negotiating and movement of positions. Although we don't know what the landlord's original positions were, we can assume he wasn't looking to give things away. Of note is the trade-off between construction costs and rent concessions. Clearly, the prospective tenant believed that an escalation of the concession period compensated for the costs of construction. It also seems likely that the perspective tenant preferred to handle the construction from the outset, but positioned it as a tradeoff for additional months of free rent.

From the landlord's perspective, the space is currently not earning revenue. Chances of getting another perspective tenant who wouldn't require renovation and alterations is remote. By giving additional concessions, the landlord avoids out-of-pocket construction costs that are considerable ($130,000 in this deal), and wins other cost savings points on security and manning the freight elevator.

CONCLUSION

We have used the example of a real estate deal to make the points in this chapter. In fact, attention to detail in the planning, initiating, and interaction phases of a negotiation carries the same importance regardless of the type of negotiation involved. Being aware and keeping track of the interaction between the various components and issues will make you a better negotiator. This perspective supports and encourages efforts at finding alternative solutions. It militates against positional and single-issue bargaining, and goes a long way toward counteracting tactics. While we have dealt with the issue of attending to detail separately from the issue of planning, it is clearly part of the planning process as well as the ongoing negotiation activity.

Notes

[1]Dennis M. Horn, *Negotiating Real Estate Transactions*, Mark A. Senn, ed. (New York: Wiley, 1988), p. 3. Reprinted by permission of John Wiley & Sons, Inc., Copyright © 1988, John Wiley & Sons, Inc.

[2]Horn, p. 7.

[3]Horn, p. 9.

[4]Horn, p. 9.

[5]Robert Lawrence Kuhn, *Dealmaker* (New York: Wiley, 1988), p. 25. Reprinted by permission of John Wiley & Sons, Inc., Copyright © 1988, John Wiley & Sons, Inc.

CHAPTER 8

Negotiating Financial Sales

The following is an excerpt from an interview conducted between the authors and the principal member of a major Wall Street research/ investment firm.

Investment Manager:

About 2 or 3 weeks ago a private company was attempting to do an initial public offering. It's a small company and they were having a problem getting enough interest to go ahead with the deal. Our analyst did his homework, and, in fact, thought that this thing represented some pretty good fundamental value. So, late in the game, we got involved and did help bring together some sizable investors.

The company has in mind a price range of $10 to $12½, but is willing to accept $10 if they had to. And, this is put on the front of a prospectus in the initial public offering—it's not set in stone or anything, it's just where they're aiming to try to do the deal. In good markets, the deal would have been done at $12½ with maybe a little premium above that. Well, we're in a market where there is a lot less interest than you'd like to have. So, even though we generated orders for 700,000 or 800,000 shares, it was a 1.5 million share offer. When the company ended its negotiations with the underwriters, the pricing was at $8. I'm sure that the guy who formed that company was sitting there faced with, "God, what do I do now? I'm not going to give my company away." On the other hand, he was highly leveraged and he had put this thing together on private financing. He needed the equity to pay down some of those back loans so they could continue building the assets of the company. When he was offered $8, he could have refused the deal and walked away. If he had not gone ahead with the offer, he would be looking at 6 weeks of marketing and the expense of printing prospectuses; the legal expenses—probably between $250,000 to $350,000—were already sunk into this thing. Second, he probably didn't have an alternative source of private financing. So, when he was faced with this news on that Tuesday at four o'clock in the afternoon, and he saw that $8 offer with the spread of 7 percent, which makes it substantially less than he wants, can he still get up and walk away from the table?

We were just staring at each other in the face and trying to guess whether the guy would accept the $8 proposal, because we also had sunk a lot into going after 4 or 5 weeks of marketing this thing. Our reputation was at stake; if the deal was not doable, we shouldn't have been there in the first place. If we try offering a higher price, the deal isn't going to work and that will also hurt our reputation. On the other hand, we don't want the deal to just disappear.

It was the perfect situation for getting up and walking away. But, the owner had his reasons for wanting to go with the public offering at that point, and he bit the bullet and said, "O.K. I don't like it, but I'll take it."

Healy:
Because it's a major point in our approach to negotiation, I'd like to stay with it for a moment. You talk about the ability to walk away. It seems to me the first rule of thumb is don't put yourself into a situation where you can't walk away.

Investment Manager:
I would put a totally positive bias on it, rather than a negative. I would say, don't get into negotiations until you have given yourself options so you can walk away—as opposed to don't go into something you can't walk away from. I mean, life isn't that way. Before you get involved with negotiations— before you get down to the nitty gritty—try and put yourself into a position where you have options so that you can walk away, because you will come away with a very different end result in the negotiations if that's the case. It's like insurance in my book. You don't want to ever use it if you don't have to because you are actually doing something positive. You want a positive conclusion to it, but you have an insurance policy in case it rains.

Life is such that you will find yourself in situations where you can't comfortably get up from the table, say "screw you," and walk out of the room. Some people will do that even when there aren't any good options. They'll do it even when the consequences of walking away are greater than accepting a less-than-perfect deal. But the question is: Are they walking away based on emotion, or rational thinking?

If they're walking away based on emotion, it's certainly an error on their part in judgment and objectivity. But, it's also an error on the part of the other negotiator. If I'm concerned about your emotion, that becomes my problem as part of how I negotiate.

Even when you seemingly have the upper hand, you have to be pretty self-effacing in a financial negotiation. In one case we put together a deal for a guy who has an understanding of himself that relates to the way he spent the last 63 years in a very narrow little cocoon in the south. He was handed a business and, like others in the same situation, after he's been in it a few years he really thinks that this is his business. He thinks that he earned it when, in fact, it was handed to him. Now he doesn't understand that he is a lousy salesman. For 6 weeks he and his chief financial officer, also a horrible salesman, have been out trying to sell investment in this company. Their actions actually had an adverse effect on the value of their security and their negotiations. Someone else in the same situation might have been smooth, and would have had some positive effect as opposed to negative. But is anyone sitting down with this guy and saying, "Look, you are the worst salesman I ever met, and it has cost you $2 or $3 a share, and it possibly cost you your ability to do the deal at all."

Gottlieb:

So, what you're saying is that in the process of his negotiation, by doing something wrong—whatever that was—in terms of his sales ability, he affected the total value of his deal."

Investment
Manager:

That's right. His investment banker isn't going to tell him. It's a professional relationship, and you just don't tell a guy that he's full of baloney if he's your client. The people who work for him aren't going to tell him. It's his company, so who's around to tell him he's making a fool out of himself?

While the preceding excerpt from an interview relates to activities surrounding initial public offerings of securities, several key points are applicable to financial services negotiations of a wide variety and to negotiation in general.

1. The importance of objectivity and the control of emotion.
2. The relationship between negotiation and salesmanship; and the need to accurately assess your sales ability and style for its potential effect on the deal.
3. The need to consider alternatives to the desired outcome.

Negotiation is a communications act. This probably doesn't land on you with the force of revelation but, as a communication construct, there are some important things to be considered. As with all communication acts, negotiation follows certain rules; some are obvious, others are subtle, and still others are downright obscure. At the simplest level, the parties involved take turns talking. They use language and other signs and symbols to develop and project meaning. At the most complex level, the parties vie for control and seek to influence each other through syntactical positioning and paralinguistic manipulation.

We have already demonstrated some of the dynamics that occur between negotiating parties as they set the rules for their interaction. As before, the selling situation provides a good backdrop for gaining an understanding of important negotiating principles.

NEGOTIATING AND SELLING

Since this chapter focuses on financial sales, it is important to discuss the relationship between sales and negotiation. Many people in financial sales have difficulty seeing themselves as salespeople. How can you negotiate and sell at the same time? In fact, while engaged in negotiation you can't forget that you are first and foremost a salesperson. Negotiation, rightly understood, is part of a larger process which contains, in addition to the negotiation component, a prospecting component, a relationship-building component, a follow-up component, and all of the other factors that go into building excellent sales performance. If you have been selling for several years, no one has to tell you that selling has changed. Chalk it up to the economy, to deregulation, competition, to merger-acquisition activity, to downsizing, or to any number of other catalysts of change in the marketplace. Certainly competition is stiffer, margins are narrower, and the buyers of your products and services are becoming increasingly professional in the way they handle their side of the issue.

In an article entitled, "Developing Consultative Sales Skills: A Formula for Excellence," Jack R. Snader posed this question: "Why do some people excel in selling products or services, while others who seem to work just as hard, and enthusiastically, fall short of meeting company or personal sales goals?"[1] He goes on to say that an audit of top sales performers from Fortune 500 and smaller entrepreneurial-based companies would likely point to one principal talent that would distinguish elite profit makers from poorer-performing peers—their ability to skillfully diagnose and solve problems better and quicker than the competition. A resourceful salesperson solves problems.

Clearly, there is a relationship between negotiation and sales, particularly where a problem-solving approach is the key to success. But, it goes beyond that. A problem solver realizes the need to understand the features, benefits, and technical aspects of the product line; but, a problem solver also recognizes that the products are not the most pressing concern, rather it is the needs of the client that are most pressing. This strategy of applying problem solving to the selling process, of determining the needs and wants of the customer is client-centered or consultative selling. These needs are not confined to product and service issues. They include the prospect's psychosocial needs and values. By identifying and serving the personalized needs of each prospect, a salesperson will match the right buyers to the right products and services more quickly and more cost-effectively.

In financial services industries, similar services are often available, or perceived to be available, from many suppliers. This makes it more obvious that buyers are more likely to favor the particular salesperson who most effectively shapes solutions to their needs. In client-centered or consultative selling we talk about being buyer oriented, about taking the time to listen to the potential buyer and ask questions to uncover needs at all levels—product needs, tastes, attitudes, and feelings. If one fault were to be selected from the observations of thousands of salespeople, it would be that they don't ask enough questions. The time the salesperson spends analyzing needs and prefer-ences by asking open, in-depth questions and evaluating the answers is productive for both parties regardless of the particular selling phase they may be in.

At another point in his article, Snader develops a useful analogy regarding understanding, credibility, and process concerns.

In consultative selling, a salesperson interacts with a prospect much as a doctor does with a patient. If one visits a doctor for lower-back pain and the doctor—following a brief discussion—prescribes surgery, one would no doubt feel apprehensive and would probably seek another opinion. However, if the physician spends time learning how the patient feels, performs a series of tests and only then draws conclusions, the patient will feel much more comfortable with the prescription because a more thorough analysis was conducted.

So it goes in selling. Just as the doctor's thorough analysis creates patient comfort with the prescription, the salesperson's thorough analysis will make a prospective buyer comfortable.[2]

A good salesperson can do more with effective questioning techniques than with a good sales pitch in establishing trust and in a sense of understanding the client's problem or need. Often, the buyer doesn't have a good understanding of his or her own needs until the salesperson uncovers them through questioning. Research indicates that there are several identifiable skills that are associated with top sales producers in a broad cross-section of industries.

1. They are good listeners, not good talkers.

2. They don't present the product or service until they uncover the needs.

3. They never begin the sales call with a presentation because that establishes one-way communication. Rather they begin with dialogue to establish a consultative approach.

4. They present only those features and benefits that relate to the prospect's needs.

5. They don't try to close until it appears that the needs have been met.

6. They don't treat resistance as an objection to be overcome. Rather, they see it as a series of questions or concerns that must be answered.

7. They believe that the client relationship begins rather than ends with the sale.

8. They set their goals beyond being a salesperson toward being a continuing resource for the client.

In fact this same list of competencies can be directed at good negotiators. It is often very difficult to draw a line between selling and negotiating when the activity is taking place. You may find as you go through this book that some of the skills being taught appear to be at odds with basic selling techniques you have already mastered. But, you will come to see that the shift is not a fundamental change in approach, but an expansion in the sales process to accommodate the demands imposed by negotiation. Rightly understood, negotiation is part of closing a sale. The client has given a clear buying signal by agreeing to negotiate with you in the first place. If you can resolve the remaining conflicts and objections, and in the process build a better relationship than that which your competitors can offer, you will close more deals.

Regular and ongoing negotiation has become an increasing part of the salesperson's job. As part of the consultative sales process, it requires a problem-solving perspective and problem-solving skills. To boost a salesperson's chances for success, he or she must be perceived and then appreciated as a problem solver.

THE SALESPERSON AND THE PURCHASING MINDSET

One of the key discoveries from our research is that among people who find themselves regularly selling and/or negotiating for a living, there is a tendency to develop stereotypes of the parties with whom they negotiate. These stereotypes provide impediments to effective problem-solving strategies or collaborative negotiation. One such situation often occurs between salespeople and purchasing people. While they are strongly interdependent in order to accomplish the tasks and responsibilities of their jobs, the nature of their relationship breeds stereotypic thinking.

Large companies will almost always involve the purchasing department in any new vendor transactions. In fact, most RFPs (request for proposal) and RFQs (request for quote) are generated through the purchasing arm of an organization. Smaller companies may go the same route, or may not have a separate purchasing function. However, someone in the organization is charged with the responsibility of acquiring the best possible deal at the lowest possible cost, and this person will inevitably be part of the negotiation process.

The situation lends itself to the development of stereotypes. Many salespeople have developed a negative stereotype of the typical purchasing person, and they tend to generalize this stereotype toward all purchasers. The word *purchasing* often raises visions of unyielding, ill-humored individuals—often pictured with a green eye-shade—who spend their lives beating people up over minutiae, who miss the larger picture, and don't enter into the give-and-take spirit of negotiation at all. This view is so pervasive that it has become encapsulated in the phrase, "purchasing mentality." A purchasing mentality, or mindset, is not confined to the people who work for purchasing departments. Anyone with whom you are negotiating, regardless of title, can exhibit it; one always knows when someone with mindset that has entered the room.

The effect of the purchasing mindset is very powerful for a number of reasons.

The person seems unreachable on a human level.

The person appears only to demand and not negotiate.

The person seems not to like you.

The person seems to have all of the authority to make the decision.

The result of this situation often makes the sales negotiator feel subservient, thus forcing the negotiator to lower his or her aspiration levels. Also, a pattern of communication is established that places the sales negotiator on the defensive. A key concept is that *power grows out of someone else's dependency*. As long as you are made to feel that you need what the other person has to give more than the other person needs what you have to give, your dependency gives power to the other person.

The purchasing stereotype grows out of some very real experience that people have had in doing business. People with this mentality generally battle their way up in an organization through the ranks. In large organizations, they rarely have advancement opportunities beyond the purchasing area. As such, they tend to guard their territory very tenaciously.

On the other hand, all purchasing professionals can tell stories that relate how they got "done-in" by a salesperson at various points in their career. They see themselves as straightforward, hard-working individuals trying to do the best for their families, their companies, and themselves. They see themselves as neither super-intelligent nor glib. They attribute their success to their attention to detail, their ability to remain unemotional in the decision-making process, and sheer stubbornness. Salespeople are viewed in the opposite manner.

Salespeople are seen as glib, untrustworthy, in-it-for-themselves individuals who will take advantage of any situation. They appear to befriend you, but they really feel superior and look down on you. When they get the best of you, they go and brag about it to other salespeople—probably other ones who call on you.

Tied to this basic view of doing business and the attitude toward salespeople is considerable ability with positional bargaining tactics—many learned the hard way—and no driving need (at least not apparent during negotiation) to be likable.

If each side enters the negotiation expecting and responding to these stereotypes, bargaining will indeed be very difficult.

Earlier we discussed the drawbacks of positional bargaining and presented the point of view that a problem-solving approach to negotiation was preferable in every instance. The purchaser fitting the profile described above is not burdened with any such enlightenment. With skill and patience, the sales negotiator can move the proceedings toward that direction.

The positional bargainer presents certain demands—usually a list (written or verbal)—at the outset of the negotiation. Success is measured in terms of how many of these demands are met at the end of the process. The stubbornness is fueled by the notion that "no deal" is better than a "bad deal," and that the positional bargainer is more likely to draw fire from the company because of a bad deal; the no deal position is more defendable from the perspective of its "not being good for the company."

Seasoned positional bargainers anticipate that there will probably need to be some compromise, so they exaggerate their opening positions. They believe that knowledge is power, and make every effort to disguise their real needs so that you can't "take advantage" of them.

ALTERNATIVES TO AGREEMENT

The concept of walking away from a deal is an elusive one for salespeople. After all, if you don't make the sale, you don't make a living. Yet, more money is lost by salespeople and the companies that employ them because of this one fear than perhaps anything else that may occur in the negotiation. There are no easy solutions to this problem. The nature of the situation and the psychology of the salesperson combine to produce this sense of weakness.

If you are burdened with the perception that you cannot afford to walk away without a deal, you are at a disadvantage and will probably be forced into making unwise or unnecessary concessions. In any negotiation you should position yourself as having more than a single option, source, contact, prospect, or availability of the goods and services under consideration. If you have alternatives, it will increase your confidence and bolster your power in the negotiation, since failing to reach an agreement with this particular party is not your last resort. Skilled negotiators always perform as though they have alternatives available. In some cases they do, in others they do not.

The best antidote for your fear of walking is to speculate on the other side's alternatives to reaching an agreement with you. Even if that purchasing agent doesn't depend on a commission for a living, he or she will have to explain why a deal couldn't be made or, worse, try to build lawn mowers or whatever without your parts, or pay more for the same thing from someone else.

A second approach is to look within. Borrow a technique from stress management and ask yourself some probing questions:

"Will I still be alive if this deal falls apart?"
Answer: Probably.

"Will I lose my family and friends?"
Answer: Probably not.

"Will I lose my job? My money? My house?"
Answer: Maybe.

In this way, you can complete a reality check. What is my greatest risk here? What will I do if it happens? By facing up to these concerns and, in effect "looking over the edge" before entering into a negotiation, you can enhance your ability to operate from a position of strength.

At the end of this chapter is a Sales Negotiation Detail Form that can be used as part of your preparation for a financial sales negotiation. The following are some of the questions that must be asked to develop your objectivity and sense of control in a negotiation.

1. How is the other party currently handling the problem under discussion?
2. How did you make contact with this person?
3· What were the events leading to this negotiation?
4. What is the name, title, age, sex, and temperament of the other negotiator(s)?
5. What are the most important issues to the other side?
6. What do you know about the other party's negotiation style?
7. Where does the matter stand now?
8. What problems have been solved? What problems remain?
9. Who is responsible for the next step?
10. Who else is involved in the outcome?

CONCLUSION

The skilled negotiator develops and maintains objectivity. This is achieved by focusing on the formality of negotiation, by seeing it as a communication act with rules and structure, and by countering stereotypical notions that are factored into the negotiation. The skilled sales negotiator understands the connection between problem solving and selling, the need to be consultative, and the need to develop relationships. Finally, skilled negotiators of any stripe enter the fray knowing an agreement is not always possible, and have their alternatives built into their plans.

Notes

[1] Jack R. Snader, "Developing Consultative Sales Skills: A Formula for Excellence," *Pace*, October 1985, p. 51. Reprinted with permission *PACE* magazine, the Piedmont Airlines in-flight magazine, Pace Communications Inc., Greensboro, NC.

[2] Snader, p. 51.

Figure 8.1. Sales Negotiation Detail Form

Prospect/Client Company Name _____
Type of Business _____
Company Size:
  Number of Employees _____
  Gross Revenues ($) _____
  Payment Methods _____

Client's Principal Products or Services:
_____
_____
_____

How Did You Make Contact (Referral, Cold Call, etc.)?
_____
_____

What Are (Were) the Events Leading to Negotiation?
_____
_____

Provide a Character Sketch of Each Buyer Involved in the Negotiation:
Buyer 1 Name _____ Title _____
  Reports to _____
  Age _____ Sex _____
  Temperament _____
  Negotiating Style _____

What Issues Are Most Important to Him/Her? _____
_____
_____

Buyer 2 Name _____ Title _____
  Reports to _____
  Age _____ Sex _____
  Temperament _____
  Negotiating Style _____

What Issues Are Most Important to Him/Her? _____
_____
_____

Buyer 3   Name _____   Title _____
Reports to _____
Age _____   Sex _____
Temperament _____
Negotiating Style _____

What Issues Are Most Important to Him/Her? _____
_____
_____
_____

Buyer 4   Name _____   Title _____
Reports to _____
Age _____   Sex _____
Temperament _____
Negotiating Style _____

What Issues Are Most Important to Him/Her? _____
_____
_____
_____

Provide a Narrative of Events During the Negotiation(s), and/or Where
the Matter Stands Now:
    What Do They Want?
    What Do We Want?
    What Problems Have Been Solved?
    What Problems Remain?
    Who Is Responsible for the Next Step?
    Who Else in Your Organization is Involved?
_____
_____
_____
_____
_____

What Is the Next Step?
    Your Goal(s) _____
    _____
    _____

    Action Plan _____
    _____
    _____
    _____
    _____

What Are Your Alternatives to Making This Deal?

_____

_____

_____

_____

_____

CHAPTER 9

Negotiating in an Intercultural Setting

The communication factors that shape a culture provide indexes for predictability. The less we are able to predict, the more uncertain we become; and we experience this as a lack of control. Even within the same culture, there is a certain amount of unpredictability. Parties and other informal gatherings provide structured opportunities for people to interact in an unpredictable manner. However, in society at large, disorganization and uncertainty are not perceived as functional.

In his book, *Communication and Behavior*, Gerhard Hanneman talks about why foreigners stand out from others.

Think of the culture in which you participate. You understand some of its character, internalize certain of its values, and constrain your social behavior accordingly. Note that the shared culture you and a friend possess already organizes or controls what behavior is tolerable. One can predict your behavior from a knowledge of what culture you are a part of. Such a social unit of behavior is the reason that foreign visitors to a new culture stand out: They are at a loss to predict the consequences of their behavior; they find it difficult to control their interactions. As a result, people in new cultures often overcompensate and may express their values ostentatiously.[1]

One is reminded of the "Ugly American" syndrome which referred to American tourists in postwar Europe. In our interview with the president and CEO of a major multinational manufacturing company, he mentioned that during a negotiation with the British, he was perceived as "pushy and impatient" for expecting to accomplish his agenda in only one visit.

For most business people it is becoming increasingly difficult to avoid intercultural negotiations. Economies, marketing strategies, and international agreements are all conspiring to lure and even demand that we negotiate with each other across national boundaries. A recent article in *American Demographics* underlined how little the vast majority of Americans know about Moslems, and then pointed out that Moslems constitute one-fifth of the world's population and are growing more rapidly than any other group "if you trade internationally, up to one-fifth of your customers are Moslems."[2]

EXPECTATIONS, CONTROL, AND CULTURAL CONTEXT

Generalizing about cultural response patterns can result in stereotyping. The examples and scenarios presented in this chapter are intended to sensitize readers to the potential pitfalls of misreading cultural cues. Certainly all Japanese, or Germans, or Swedes will not respond identically to the same situations, neither would all Americans. But, the skillful negotiator will consider cultural differences as an important part of the overall approach used in the negotiation process.

In the following excerpt from an interview with the president and CEO of a multinational manufacturing company, he shares with us his experiences in doing business with foreign cultures, particularly his experiences in the Orient. He raises central issues that anyone would confront when negotiating with people from another culture.

CEO: Negotiation, as most of us think of it, is a concept of Western business, Western family, Western whatever. . . . If you contrast this attitude with a more tribal culture you get a different picture. Primitive cultures coming out of a tribal background do not come out with negotiating skill because it is a foreign concept to them. If the head of the tribe said "You will," no one said back, "What do you think?" So, the first question you should ask yourself when you are negotiating with a different culture is, "Does the concept of negotiation exist within their cultural background?"

Who were some of the best negotiators during our time? The Irish. Any special reason? They were people who were living under the control of England; forced to conduct their affairs in a sub-rosa manner in order to exist. They couldn't present anything in "definites." Here were Roman Catholics operating under the Church of England, and in order to survive they became masters of negotiation. When they came to the United States, they already had language on their side—so they were very successful negotiators in politics and unions.

Even within this country there are cultural differences related to an inherent understanding of the negotiating process. Many special interest groups in this country have become very good at confrontation. Over the last 25 years they have brought confrontation to a high point—but not negotiation. So they make extreme demands, get attention focused on the issue, and rather than solving the problem, they more likely end in a stalemate where no one wins.

As you know, I have had considerable negotiations with the Japanese and Koreans recently. If you take a look at the Japanese cultural foundations, you see a patriarchy that reveres family and elders. If Dad said, "You will not . . ." the response wasn't, "Gee, Dad, let me give you my side of it."

Each culture has its own response patterns to conflict. So, when you enter into negotiation, which is perhaps the highest form of interpersonal relationship between groups, you then ask questions of yourself that shape your expectations about what will happen during the negotiating process. In England, decisions have to be made very far up the line. In Latin America, machismo dictates that one establish one's turf. "If I accept your deal, I'm that much less a man." Negotiation is very individualistic.

The things that I have found that are unique in the Japanese culture revolve around the Japanese pride in sameness. When you get into negotiation, you don't negotiate as individuals as you and I might. It is rather your company negotiating with my company. Your people negotiating with my people.

Gottlieb:	Why do they find it necessary to involve so many people?
CEO:	They have this concept of lifetime employment. This means that you don't screw up and have a blot on your copy book for the rest of your career. Therefore, the first rule in Japan is, "No surprises, safe decisions." When we were looking at a joint venture, we showed them a building that met all of the requirements they laid out—the roof height and everything else. The plant manager said that it would be perfect, but he couldn't recommend it. I said, "Why not? It's half the price of new construction." He said, "Can you guarantee that there are no cracks in the floor or that nothing will go wrong with the building?" I said, "Well, of course not." He said, "I have to. I have to give that as a guarantee. What would happen if we moved in there and the floor started to crumble?" So, his position was to make the safe decision and build a new building. Then you know everything will be right.
Gottlieb:	Even at twice the money?
CEO:	Yes. But it was actually three times the money because it came down to, "Do you want to be located in Pennsylvania?" And his first question was, "How many Japanese businesses are here?" It turns out that the highest concentration of Japanese businesses are along Interstate 75 from Atlanta to Nashville. "We need to be in that corridor," he said, "because all the

others are there." The feeling was that if they made the decision that this was the right place, then we should make the same decision.

Another major question to ask is, "At what level does major negotiation take place?" If you and I have a dispute, it is not beyond you to call me up and say, "Let's resolve this." For the Japanese, negotiation starts at the lowest level. It would be your lieutenants talking to my lieutenants. So that by the time the presidents of the companies get together, everything would have already been done "behind the back." Negotiations take place at that level because there is nothing gained or lost, since the negotiators are not empowered to make decisions.

One of my problems was that I would come in as the president of a company, expecting the president of a Japanese company to say, "Yes, I will make a decision." But, he would not make a decision, because if he made the wrong one he would lose prestige or otherwise suffer humiliating consequences.

The next problem in negotiating with the Japanese is the word "no." The word in Japanese is much harder to say than the word "yes," and it is a culture that is built on politeness. If I asked, "Do you have any bananas?" The answer is, "Yes, I have no bananas." Everything is answered in what seems to be a positive, when really they are saying negative. "It is very difficult," translates as, "That's impossible to do." "Hard to say," means, "Forget it." They just won't come out and say no because they are attempting to be very polite.

Another factor that influences negotiation with the Japanese is that they don't relate to profit incentive the same way we do. They draw up a master plan that is usually 1 year, 2 years or even 5 years down the road. They are not bothered as much by how they perform on the short term, but how well they are doing against long-term plans. Japanese stock analysis focuses on how the company is doing against long-

term global goals. The Japanese had a commitment to
sell X amount of product in the United States regardless of whether the yen was at 250 or at 110. They
still lived up to their plans. The major companies did
not pull out of here.

Gottlieb: What about tactics?

CEO: They are basically unresponsive to tactics. "Good
guy-bad guy, take it or leave it . . ." these are concepts that don't exist for them. Incidentally, I will
point out to you that they have been bargaining for a
long time, and they bargain like they have all the
time in the world. "If not this century, then the
next."

Gottlieb: If you were to ask yourself five questions that would
help you prepare for a negotiation with the Japanese,
what would they be?

CEO: Number one would be, "How far am I willing to go on
the major points of this negotiation?" Write down
the farthest you're willing to go. Be prepared to walk
away.

Two is, "How can I structure each issue so that the
other side perceives the situation as win-win?"

Third is, "Who am I negotiating with? Who has
the real power to make particular decisions despite
the title they hold?"

Fourth, "How much time can I allot for the negotiating process?" Never negotiate with fixed time
limits. Negotiation in the Orient gets serious 1 hour
before you are getting on your plane. If you set fixed
time limits, they will believe that you don't believe
the negotiation is important.

Fifth, "What can be trusted to speech, and what
must be written down?" Any proposals should be
submitted in writing. Their reading comprehension
of English is much greater than their understanding of
spoken English. They also appreciate the opportunity
to study a proposal in detail.

THE ROLE OF LANGUAGE

Language, rightly understood, is a sequence of symbols strung together in a pattern. These symbols or words do not have meaning in and of themselves. If two people grow up in the same culture and know the English language, they can probably agree on the meaning attached to a particular symbol. If the symbol is *denotative*, like the word "door," agreement can be achieved easily. If, however, the symbol is abstract or *connotative* such as the word "agreement," "compromise," or "reasonable," there can be substantial difficulty agreeing on the meaning. We use the term "collaborate" often in this book to describe a mindset and approach to negotiation that is inherently positive. However, a native of France might perceive collaboration as negative because of that country's cultural experience with collaborators during World War II.

The meanings are not in the words, they are in the people. Cross-cultural communication has severe difficulties because participants don't share each other's background and experiences. One solution is to use and agree on dictionary definitions. However, there are drawbacks to this as well. Many words have multiple meanings.

One thing for the intercultural negotiator to be sensitive to is how language shapes the attitudes and perceptions of the speakers of that language. Researchers claim that Eskimos actually see many different kinds of snow because they have words in their language to describe the phenomena. Native American Indian cultures are patterned very differently from mainstream North American culture based on patterns in their language. Nootka, a language of the Native Americans of Vancouver Island, makes no distinction between nouns and verbs. Nootka speakers see the world as a constant process, which is constantly changing, whereas English speakers see things as fixed or constant. In Nootka, a "fire" might be described as "burning," a "house" as "housing." English trains us to see things as static and unchanging. Nootka trains speakers of that language to see things in a constant state of change.

Most of us will not be negotiating with Native American Vancouver Islanders, but the principle applies to more familiar languages as well. When a child is mischievous, an English-speaking parent will label the behavior "bad." French parents will say, "*Sois sage*," meaning "be wise." So, to the French, the act of misbehaving is foolishness.

Swedes would say *"Var snell"* or "be friendly," "be kind." Germans would command, *"Sei artig,"* meaning "get back into step and conform to your expectations as a child."

While language is only one factor that shapes our ability to communicate across cultures, it ranks as the most important. In many countries it is advisable to have a translator on site during any business negotiations. Obviously, this means that the translator must be briefed on your objectives, and understand your approach to the negotiation. Sometimes the selection of one word over another can make the difference in losing or gaining a point or the entire deal.

The ancient Japanese tied space and social organization together. Shoguns arranged the daimyo, or nobles, in concentric zones around the capital. Proximity to the center of the circle reflected a noble's relationship with the shogun. Those who were farthest away were less trusted. The concept of closeness and the ability to be approached from all directions is central to understanding how the Japanese function. Some Japanese companies use variations of this principle when setting up their office structures.

All generalizations must be tempered with good solid observation, common sense, and attention to the unique character of each negotiation. However, having considered these notions as part of your planning process, and having used them as guideposts along the way in helping you to interpret a specific interaction or frame an appropriate response, you are no doubt in better control than you would be had you not considered them.

PLANNING, PATTERNS OF COMMUNICATION, INTERPRETING CULTURAL DIFFERENCES, AND THE PERCEPTION AND USE OF POWER

The question is, how much do cultural issues affect negotiation? The answer: more than one chapter can cover. It is not our purpose to point out detailed negotiating factors in every intercultural situation. However, there are several factors that are common to all intercultural negotiations regardless of the country or people involved. The skilled negotiator is sensitive to how these factors influence several important aspects of the process including planning, patterns of communication, and the perception and use of power.

Planning

All of the points made in Chapter 6 about the importance of planning are applicable in intercultural negotiation. The main objective is, as always, to gain control over as many variables as possible. The intercultural element introduces several new elements. Let's review our checklist from Chapter 6. The highlighted items are particularly affected by intercultural elements.

1. When is the negotiation taking place?
2. *How much time do you have to reach a conclusion?*
3. What are the issues to be negotiated?
4. *What are the issues to be avoided?*
5. How should the issues be prioritized?
6. How is each issue valued?
7. *Negotiate as a team or individually?*
8. What are your authority limits?
9. What are the facts?
10. *What is the other side's point of view?*
11. What do I know about the other negotiatior(s)?
12. *What outside influences may affect the negotiation?*
13. What are your acceptable ranges for the deal?
14. What is your plan of action?
15. Have you used roleplay to practice your approach?

Of the 15 items on the list, four are particularly sensitive. Time is an example. As our CEO says in his interview, "You can't give the impression to a Japanese, Korean, or British negotiator that you are in a hurry. The Oriental will interpret this as a lack of seriousness on your part. The Englishman will interpret this as pushy and unrealistic."

In Belgium, the first meeting is to get acquainted. You should be prepared to answer questions about yourself. Belgians need to trust you personally before they will have confidence in your company. German business people also spend some time on general conversation before getting down to business. As with other Europeans, Germans operate more slowly than Americans. They believe that a good job requires time, and they proceed in a very deliberate manner. In fact, Germans generally don't trust the quality of businesses which specialize in fast service. German observation of Americans is that Americans are very structured in their use of time, that they are sticklers for schedules, they schedule too many events in any period of time, and leave little free time for themselves. Europeans in general see Americans as more concerned with the schedule than with personal relationships.

In Austria, it is permissible to be up to 15 minutes late for a business appointment. In Greece, you are expected to be punctual, but this isn't reciprocal. Portuguese are very tolerant if you are late, and are generally 15 to 30 minutes late themselves. However, in Denmark it is very important for all parties to be exactly on time, as it is in Germany, Italy, Finland, and Sweden. It is very difficult to do business anywhere in Europe during July and August, since most business people plan their vacations during those months.

Anyone negotiating with a different culture must be supersensitive to issues that should be avoided or deferred to at a different time or with a different person. The Japanese, as noted earlier, cover all of the substantive issues at the lowest possible level. When the "decision makers" sit down at the table, all of the terms of the agreement should have been settled. By contrast, in Finland and other European countries, negotiation should be initiated at the highest levels. You can gauge how a negotiation is going by who is assigned to meet with you. If there is a problem, you will see lower-level people. The English have a phrase that goes, "Why keep dogs if you have to do your own barking." In Greece, a negotiation can go on for a very long time because Greeks work out all of the details of a business arrangement with everyone who is affected by the arrangement present in the room, and they will continue the meeting as long as is necessary to come to an agreement.

It is difficult enough to analyze the other party's point of view when you share a common culture. The difficulty is compounded when the two sides come from a totally different cultural orientation. Ask yourself, what issues may or may not be of particular importance to my counterparts purely on cultural grounds? The Japanese put a premium on being with other Japanese in any plans they make for international development. The Germans associate deliberateness with quality. The Koreans are particularly interested in your company's references for establishing a business relationship. Latin Americans tie their self-esteem into winning points for their side, and are much more difficult to deal with in a collaborative way.

Many of the same outside influences have an effect on intercultural and intracultural negotiation: business and economic conditions, demand, supply, competition, and so forth. Here, the question to ask is, what cultural factors may be influencing the behavior and perceptions of the other negotiator? The Japanese feel they must play it safe and avoid the risk of losing face. Latin Americans are also concerned with losing face, but rather than playing it safe, they want to score points. The Dutch are intolerant of spontaneity. So, the "Let's be creative and all work this out together right here and now," approach will not go over well.

Patterns of Communication

Negotiation depends on effective communication taking place between the parties involved. As you would expect, the culture one grows up in shapes the patterns of one's communication in very different and important ways. The observations of Edward Hall in his classic work, *The Hidden Dimension*, should be required reading for anyone who needs to develop the sensitivity to relate interpersonally with other cultures.

For example, Hall points out that "public school" upper class English have a greater capacity to direct and modulate the voice than do Americans; they become very annoyed when there is acoustic interference because noise makes it difficult for them to apply this vocal skill. Of equal importance is what people tend to screen out of their perceptions.

People brought up in different cultures learn as children, without ever knowing that they have done so, to screen out one type of information while paying close attention to another. Once set, these perceptual patterns apparently remain quite stable throughout life. The Japanese, for example, screen visually in a variety of ways but are perfectly content with paper walls as acoustic screens. Spending the night at a Japanese inn while a party is going on next door is a new sensory experience for the Westerner. In contrast, the Germans and the Dutch depend on thick walls and double doors to screen sound, and have must rely on their own powers of concentration to screen out sound. If two rooms are the same size and one screens out sound but the other one doesn't, the sensitive German who is trying to concentrate will feel less crowded in the former because he feels less intruded on.[3]

The Negotiation Planning Form in Chapter 6 asks you to consider the location of the negotiation. The culture with whom you are negotiating may help you determine the best place to meet.

Managing the olfactory sense is particularly difficult for Americans conducting negotiation in the Middle East. Arabs apparently recognize a relationship between disposition and smell, and use the sense to detect anger or discontent. They also tend to bathe one in their breath. An American, taught not to breathe on people, finds the intensity and sensuality overwhelming—particularly in a public setting—and has trouble paying attention to what is being said. The problems this poses for negotiations is obvious.

It is basic to communication that comprehension on a high level is dependent on redundancy. Information received by one system (e.g., the eyes) is backed up by information received through another system (e.g., the ears or touch). Interpersonally, we back up our perceptions by mirroring our understanding to one another. Whenever people talk, as in negotiation, they supply only part of the message. The rest is filled in by the listener. Much of what is not said is taken for granted. However, Hall tells us,

cultures vary in what is left unsaid. To an American, it is superfluous to have to indicate to a shoeshine boy the color of the paste to be used. But in Japan, Americans who do not indicate this may send out brown shoes only to have them returned black![4]

Recent research in the area of persuasion suggests that presenters can increase their success in building rapport by determining which of three categories the other party falls into: people oriented, detail oriented, or results oriented. Once determined, the presenter (salesperson, negotiator, etc.) mirrors behaviors that suggests he or she falls into the same category. The receiver believes that their communication patterns are in sync, thus raising the comfort level.

Patterns of communication are also found in the way we use space, or the distance we place between ourselves and others. Americans are uncomfortable when they perceive that foreigners are positioned inappropriately close. The proximity creates distortion in the visual system. Middle Easterners, when describing how they won a point, will often say, "I stayed in his face."

As distance becomes greater between the parties, the voice naturally becomes louder. However, Hall made the observation that the volume of an American voice is below that of the Arab, the Spaniard, the South Asian Indian, and the Russian, while being somewhat above that of the English upper class, the Southeast Asian, and the Japanese.

Interpreting Cultural Differences

As the world gets "smaller" through technological advances in communication and contact necessitated by the globalization of business, contact between cultures—and negotiation between cultures—intensifies. Sophisticated business professionals from all cultures pride themselves on their ability to interpret other cultures. Or, to put it another way, the Americans have an opinion about how to do business with the Japanese, the French have an opinion about how to do business with the Germans, and the English have an opinion about how to do business with everyone. Behavior that is out of context in cultural terms is usually interpreted as having bad manners, or fitting into a negative stereotype, or lacking seriousness, when it is probably just the product of a misunderstanding.

At the beginning of this chapter, a CEO shared some generalizations he made from his experience in dealing with other cultures, primarily the Japanese and Koreans. Will every Japanese company respond in the same way? Probably not. Still, we are much better off if we are to be able to anticipate such responses than if we were to be caught off guard or, worse, to be confused and offensive.

Many Northern Europeans, specifically the Germans, feel they don't know where they stand when dealing with Americans. They don't like our informal attitude toward boundaries and authority in general. It would be an affront to a German to change the position of your chair during a negotiation. Hitching up your chair causes you to intrude on most Germans' private space. Chairs in Germany and other parts of Europe are made unusually heavy to discourage moving them around. Conversely, Americans believe Germans are overly rigid and formal; Germans are often misinterpreted as being arrogant or having a superiority complex.

Differences between people who speak the same language appear more subtle. Americans find English pronunciation affected. The English find some American dialects uncultured. The greatest differences occur in handling time, space, and materials. Americans use space as a way of classifying people—where you live, what office you occupy. The English are classified by their social system. As Hall puts it, If an Englishman is a Lord. "He is still a Lord—no matter where you find him, even if it is behind the counter in a fishmonger's stall."[5]

The English relate differently to space than do Americans. English childhood patterns are formed around shared rather than individual space. Typical middle-class American children think it's their right to have their own room. An Englishman may never have a permanent space of his own. Even members of Parliament do not have their own offices. If an American is angry or wishes not to be intruded upon, he or she goes into a room and closes the door. The English retreat behind a complex network of subtle cues meant to let everyone know that they do not wish to be disturbed. Problems arise when Americans don't pick up on these cues and think that they must pursue the real feelings behind what they perceive to be a major rejection. Translated into negotiation terms, an American may interpret an Englishman's unwillingness to communicate as a stone walling, or tactical behavior (secret agent), and may frame an inappropriate response which then causes further problems.

The word privacy does not exist in Japanese. The Japanese prefer or, at least, tolerate a degree of crowding. Yet, they are very conscious of private space. Their skill with creating wonderful gardens stems, in part, from their conceptualization of the spaces between objects as being part of the form, rather than as an interval between the objects. As in their gardening, the Japanese have developed an approach to relationships that leads an individual to a spot where he can discover something for himself. The negotiator who is focused on looking for something explicit, as a sign, from the Japanese may miss what is implicit.

Another example is the telephone. The English see this invention as intrusive and used for emergencies; their tendency is to write or telegram. The recent advent of the fax machine has been widely embraced by English businesses because it has the efficiency of the phone without its intrusiveness. Picking up the phone and calling an English party in a negotiation to settle a small point may be interpreted as pushy or rude.

Cultural differences with regard to the use of the voice can have an effect on the dynamics of a negotiation. In Europe, Americans are perceived as talking too loud; they are not concerned about being overheard and, in fact, use being overheard as an indication of their openness and honesty. The English have developed their ability to focus their voices and to speak just above the level of the background noise, so as not to intrude on others. Americans often interpret this as conspiratorial.

Listening behavior varies as well. English tend to blink as an indication that they have heard what you said, Americans nod and make noises. The French move in closer and look directly at you. The Arab comes even closer, and looks you in the eye with an intensity most Americans consider uncomfortable.

The Perception and Use of Power

In Chapter 2 we discussed the use and abuse of power at great length. Again, as with planning, much of the same advice holds true for intercultural negotiation as it does for negotiation in general. Power exercised in inappropriate ways can be risky or costly and can irreparably damage business relationships between the parties involved. Recall the sources of power we considered:

Risk

Knowledge/information

Expertise

Reward/punishment

Legitimate/positional

Identification/association

Referent/moral

As always, there is probably no such thing as too much information and knowledge. However, when entering an intercultural negotiation, part of the information and knowledge you must bring with you should consist of cultural factors. Protecting yourself from the assumption that others will react in prescribed ways based on your cultural experience moves you way ahead in the probability of successfully achieving your objectives.

Expertise will be a powerful tool for those that see it as a priority. On balance, everyone who is party to a business deal has to have some confidence that you can handle your end, or that you know what you're talking about. However, a German is going to place more emphasis on your apparent competence as demonstrated by your approach to the proceedings than a Japanese negotiator would. The Japanese negotiator will be less concerned with process and more concerned with how the issues fit in with previous experience.

The same parameters hold true for reward and punishment. If someone perceives that you can either reward or punish them as a result of the negotiation's outcome, they will most likely be responsive. In the intercultural mode, however, there may not be a consensus among the negotiators about what makes a reward or punishment. In recent negotiations with the Navajo Nation, the Department of the Interior offered to build and deliver brand new modern houses to Navajos willing to relocate from lands awarded to the Hopi through a court decision. The Navajos were living in hogans (somewhat equivalent to mud huts). What the government saw as a reward, the Navajos saw as a punishment, since the houses were faced the wrong way (Navajo dwellings must face east), and constructed in such a manner that they would be out of touch with the earth (a central concept in their beliefs).

Legitimate, or positional, power is very important to the English and other Northern Europeans. There is great concern in business that one speaks only to others at the same level. However, the Japanese demonstrate less concern and, in fact, the real decision maker may be fairly far down on the totem pole in American terms; as the CEO we spoke with pointed out, the issue of where to set up a manufacturing operation was decided by the plant manager not the chairman of the company.

Identification can be a great source of power. In some cases you will find it very difficult, if not impossible, to do business unless you have the proper introductions and associations. In Spain it is always advisable to use a Spanish contact to help you cultivate a relationship with business people or government officials. Spaniards value personal influence, and accomplishing anything on your own will be very difficult. If your company is well known, this can both help and hinder your efforts, depending on who the other party is and what cultural background they come from. A large company trying to set up an operation in Europe may be looked on favorably by some cultures; in Latin and Central America such a company may be viewed as having American imperialistic tendencies.

Regardless of the culture you are negotiating with, your greatest source of power will come from the referent or moral side. The normal concerns that negotiators bring with them to the table (e.g., Can I trust this person? What recourse do I have if the deal goes sour?) become amplified in the intercultural situation. National rivalries, cultural differences, and racial and ethnic animosities can and do inhibit the free flow of collaboration and problem-solving activity between the parties involved. Negotiators who have earned a very positive reputation for being fair and open, who have demonstrated a sensitivity to the idiosyncrasies of the other culture, exert a great deal of power in a negotiation. One thinks of Armand Hammer's long-standing relationship with the Soviet Union.

With regard to the power of risk, one might say that any inter-cultural negotiation carries with it risks that are difficult to anticipate. Often, such negotiations are carried on far from home over a pro-tracted period of time and at great expense. These factors make it even harder to walk away from a deal that really doesn't match our needs.

With the globalization of markets many of us will have little choice but to enter into the intercultural fray. Americans have difficulty relating to what they perceive as a lack of urgency on the part of most negotiators from other countries. One often gets the sense when dealing with Orientals or Arabs (and until recently with the English) that if the deal doesn't get done in this century, the next century would be fine.

Since time and urgency are the root of most tactics, they become ineffective in an intercultural negotiation. Having tried a "take it or leave it" and walked out of the room in a negotiation with the Koreans, the CEO we interviewed says he returned the following day and was asked, "Are you going to stay today?"

CONCLUSION

Where is your power in an intercultural negotiation? It begins with your willingness to negotiate, to tackle the very special problems that come with dealing in foreign tongues and "strange" ways. Everything on the personal side of the ledger will be intensified: Who you are; what you represent; who you know; how you present yourself; and how sensitive you are to the nuances of the other culture. As was said earlier, it is impossible to cover all of these nuances in a single chapter—perhaps even a single book—but there are some general guidelines to be followed when preparing for and entering into an intercultural negotiation.

1. *Do Your Homework!* Learn whatever you can about the culture. Go to the library. Speak to people who have had dealings with that culture. Pick up some travel guides at a bookstore since they are often the best source of cultural idiosyncrasies. Talk to American counterparts who have done business in the country where you will be negotiating and learn from their experience.

2. *Plan Your Deal Carefully.* Know the deal ranges that are acceptable, but generate as many possible combinations as possible. Things that you may deem unimportant in a negotiation may be the very items that swing the deal. Don't give them away. Use them as tradeoffs.

3. *Make Your Best Time Estimate and Then Throw It Away.* If you must negotiate within fixed time limits, you will probably be at a definite disadvantage; needless to say, you will become frustrated and end up with less than what you really want.

4. *Be Prepared to Present Much of Your Material in Writing.* Even though your counterparts appear to be fluent in English, they are still operating in a second language. They will demand the opportunity to study any fine points in detail. Offering to put your proposals in writing, and providing daily written summaries of your understanding of where the negotiation is going will build a sense of good will and raise your credibility.

5. *Use a Translator.* If there is any doubt in your mind that the other parties will be completely comfortable in English, you should use a translator.

6. *Make an Effort to Mirror Aspects of the Culture that Are Easy for You to Affect.* These include: greeting behaviors, spatial considerations, and other communication patterns. Most cultures will be flattered, or at least positively amused, if you try to use some words and phrases in their language. The exception is the French, who would rather stumble along in English than have to listen to poorly spoken French.

7. *Acknowledge Cultural Differences.* Demonstrate a willingness to speak freely about variances in behavior, expectations, and perceptions that exist between yourself and the people from another culture. Be careful to be respectful and not critical of their behaviors. Rather, indicate a willingness and a curiosity to learn. Be as candid and as clear as you can in answering questions about the way you behave.

8. *Give Special Consideration to Timing.* Consider the needs of the other party. Does the culture demand that you get better acquainted before business begins? Are you expected to share some food, drink, or gifts. What issues should be avoided in the early stages of negotiation? Avoided altogether?

9. *Be Empathic.* Try to view the situation through the eyes of the other negotiator. What are you doing that could be confusing? What assumptions are you making? Call into question everything that you view as implicit.

10. *Be Collaborative.* Try to position each negotiation as a "no-lose" situation. Keep your eyes and the eyes of your counterpart focused on the need to solve a specific set of problems. While doing so, keep in mind that at least some of the problems that need to be solved relate to cultural differences.

Notes

[1]Gerhard J. Hanneman, *Communication and Behavior* (Reading, MA: Addison-Wesley, 1975), pp. 23–24. Reprinted by permission of McGraw-Hill, Inc.

[2]"The Real Islamic Revolution," *American Demographics*, September 1989, p. 5.

[3]Edward T. Hall, *The Hidden Dimension* (Garden City, NY: Doubleday, 1966), p. 43.

[4]Hall, p. 96.

[5]Hall, p. 130.

CHAPTER 10

Why Study Negotiation?

The major task of this chapter is to summarize, amplify, and provide a rationale for the principles and practices presented in this book. We began with the notion that negotiation is an important part of every-day life, that far more things which we encounter from moment to moment are negotiable than we may think. Our research and experience have shown that most people fail to recognize potential negotiation situations.

Another issue concerns the complexity of negotiation. It must be viewed as a multilevel process which incorporates communicational, situational, psychological, and cultural variables. Much that we have learned about negotiation resides in the unconscious. We just go into a situation and do it because it feels natural for us to do it in a particular way. These preconceived ideas about what works best for us make up our style, which may or may not be appropriate in any given negotiation depending on the situation and the style of the other negotiator. Studying negotiation takes these unconscious things and places them on a conscious level, and provides us with a process through which, and by which, we can actually become more effective negotiators.

Do we mean that in every situation, having read this book, you are going to get an extra $10,000 on the deal, that you will buy a car for less, sell a house for more, win every point? No. What we're talking about are incremental gains that, over time, add up to a significant difference in your overall experience with negotiation. Satisfaction in any negotiated outcome is a relative phenomenon. If this book has provoked you to consider whether or not you are getting the best possible outcomes from your negotiations, it has succeeded in developing awareness.

At various points we talk about developing a problem-solving mindset, about being more collaborative in your approach and style. Can we solve problems and negotiate at the same time? Yes, as long as we view negotiation, in Webster's terms, as a "conference" rather than a contest. In our view, there is no substantive difference between collaborative negotiation and creative problem solving that involves more than one person. They are perceived as different because problem solving is initiated by the need to solve a problem, negotiation is initiated by conflict. However, in both instances, the solution to a problem also resolves the conflict.

No negotiated settlement will achieve agreement unless at least one party, or preferably both parties, has his underlying needs met. There tends to be a disproportionate amount of time spent defending or asserting individual points of view rather than exploring and discovering each other's real needs, and figuring out how those needs can best be satisfied. It is worth repeating: The most successful negotiators are those who focus on questions and strategies to determine and demonstrate an understanding of the other's position, including both psychosocial aspects of the interaction as well as the substance of the deal (collaborative-S1 approach). Less effective negotiation results are attributed to overbearing tactical behavior (S4), conflict avoidance (S3), or patronizing agreement to win a concession (S2).

We offer the following principles as guidelines. Although we use the device of calling them the "Gottlieb/Healy Principles," we don't mean to suggest that they are irrefutable. They represent our best interpretation of our extensive research and experience.

GOTTLIEB/HEALY PRINCIPLES

First Principle: The Greatest Failure in Negotiation Is Failing to Negotiate

Look for opportunities to apply collaborative negotiation rather than passively accepting someone's offer, withdrawing, or immediately looking for a compromise position.

Second Principle: The Most Important Person to Know in a Negotiation Is Yourself

Become aware of your predominant behavior in a negotiation. Alter your style to fit the needs of the situation, with a eye toward becoming more collaborative.

Third Principle: Everyone Has Power in a Negotiation

Understand your own source of power in a negotiation. If someone is willing to negotiate with you, you are not powerless. If you were powerless, you would simply be ordered to do something.

Prior to entering into a negotiation, know clearly the limits regarding how far you can go in making specific concessions and under what circumstances you will need to check back with your organization. To the extent possible, know, ask for, or estimate the limits of the other party with whom you are negotiating. Do not be put off by the feeling that they can make all of their decisions and you need to check back with others in your organization. It is important to learn how to use this "checking back" as an asset rather than a liability. If, in fact, you have the ultimate ability to decide on a concession, avoid being forced into making a single-issue commitment which you may regret later when you find out that more concessions will be required to make this deal happen.

Fourth Principle: Single-Issue Bargaining Leaves Both Parties Unsatisfied

All of the components of a deal must be kept open until the very end. This promotes the development of creative alternatives, and helps to ensure that the deal satisfies the substantive needs of both parties.

Efforts must constantly be made through negotiations to raise the level of decision or the focus of the problem. For example, negotiations centered on the cost of the new copier may miss the bigger or better opportunities to negotiate the issue of what is the best way to handle our office's duplication requirements. Focusing on the second situation allows for the consideration of outside duplication, multiple units, and other alternatives. Working on just the price with the salesperson of a similar copier may get you the price on that particular copier, however, it may not suitably address your real needs.

Constantly look for and force yourself and the other party to identify and seriously consider more options than are normally considered. This encourages comparison of alternatives. In addition, it may identify other issues which can be favorable to both parties, and perhaps identify or allow concessions on other issues to be made. For example, negotiating whether implementation should occur on January 1, or January 15, may preclude consideration of other dates or other significant market factors which may force an implementation earlier than January 1, or significantly later than January.

Fifth Principle: Urgency Drives Decisions

Time is a powerful force in negotiation. If you have a deadline, you have urgency to close a deal. If you have more urgency than the other party, you are in a weaker position. If you can build a sense of urgency into a negotiation, you can motivate the other party toward making a decision.

Never signal your own limitations on time. It will put you at a distinct disadvantage. The longer a negotiation continues the more likely an agreement will be reached. However, the outcome of the negotiation still favors the party with more time in which to negotiate.

Sixth Principle: Agreement Is the End;
Tradeoff Is the Means

There are many variables surrounding concessions in negotiation. Some of these include the following points.

Rate: How quickly am I willing to make concessions?

Increments: How large a concession on a given issue is the negotiator willing to make?

Quid pro quo: Placed in a position of being required to make a concession, at what point do we attempt to receive something in return? The point here is don't be forced into giving too many concessions without asking for a concession in return. Don't wait until you've given just about all you have to give before slowing down the concession and seeking answers from the other negotiator by requiring some concessions on his part.

Avoid being shamed into concessions, "Come on now, you've got to be able to do this one little thing . . . ," "Don't be so petty, in the scheme of things you have to be able to do this for us."

Don't be afraid or reluctant to "nickel and dime" on issues as they come up. First, the other negotiator will often have no reluctance to do this to you, and second, it will slow down their request for concessions.

The value of any service or concession offered diminishes rapidly after the point at which it was rendered or conceded to. If you make a concession, the value of that concession is unlikely to be any higher than at the time you made it. Therefore, request a counter-concession (quid pro quo) as soon as possible thereafter.

Seventh Principle: Even in a Collaborative Environment, Best Results Are Obtained by Keeping the Other Party on a "Need-to-Know" Basis

Be very careful about the information that you provide to the other party in a negotiation; the wrong information can be used against you. For example, tipping your hand about how important a particular delivery date is, or how desperately you need whatever it is that you are negotiating for can have significant impact on the cost of the item. Always avoid signaling anything to do with your own deadline. However, always look for signs and signals regarding the other party's approaching deadline.

Eighth Principle: The Value of Something Is Always in the Eye of the Beholder

Anticipate that certain things that are low-value tradeoffs for you, may have significant value to the other side. The true value of any point in bargaining is its value to the other party, not its value to you. The value of a concession needs to be determined before it's offered.

Once offered, it is difficult, if not impossible, to revalue a concession. Offer only concessions that meet an agreed need, otherwise you are giving away potentially valuable points and receiving nothing. Save some concessions for later in the process.

Ninth Principle: Success in Negotiation Is Directly Related to the Amount and Kind of Preparation Preceding the Negotiation

Certainly, there is not enough we can say about the importance of planning. In fact, the necessary awareness, sensitivity, understanding or perception of style, knowledge of your limitations and power, the ranges of your deal, and the value of your concessions or tradeoffs, are all affected by how well you do your homework. When all is said and done in a negotiation, you can never be overprepared.

Tenth Principle: The Ability to Walk Away or Select Another Alternative to a Negotiated Agreement Puts a Negotiator in a Very Strong Position

Negotiation should be viewed as a positive approach to resolving a conflict. So, the concern with the ability to walk away shouldn't be perceived as a negative mindset. On the other hand, unless you have "looked over the edge" as part of your preparation, you are truly not prepared to negotiate. You have to speculate on the outcome if you don't succeed in getting the deal you need. Face up to the consequences of a "no deal" situation. Keep in mind that the short-term loss of a commission, the house not bought or sold, the space not leased— painful as they may appear to be—are probably easier to swallow than the long-term effects of a bad deal.

The time to realize that you have limited options is not when you are sitting at the bargaining table. Having options provides confidence and the freedom to be collaborative.

Eleventh Principle: Even When Two Sides Are Far Apart on Major Issues, There Are Always Things They Can Agree Upon

Regardless of how large an apparent difference is, be willing to explore the other side's rationale and needs. Look for opportunities to build on areas of agreement. Don't be intimidated by their facts, figures, authority, or position. If you have completed proper prenegotiation planning, you should have confidence in your negotiation and have command of the important and relevant information. Don't dilute arguments with extraneous information or apologize for position or authority limitations.

Twelfth Principle: Meaningful Negotiation Involves Conflicts. The Person Who Has a Strong Need to Be Liked, or Who Tends to Avoid Conflict, Is Likely to Be at a Disadvantage

Remember that being collaborative doesn't necessarily mean being "Mr. Nice Guy" all the time. Keep your focus on what negotiation is: An effective means for resolving conflict through the satisfaction of the substantive and relationship needs of the parties involved. Watch for and counter noncollaborative tactics. In most instances, it isn't necessary to abandon your collaborative approach. In fact, continuing to press for problem-solving activity in the presence of tactical maneuvering is often a potent antidote.

CONCLUSION

We have tried to shed some light on the processes and techniques of negotiation. Hopefully, we have created some awareness and insight that is applicable to your need for negotiation. The complexity of human interaction does not yield easily to analysis or formulas. Be prepared, but don't expect that you can predict the outcome of a negotiation. Even when the results appear to be crucial, you have to be open, flexible, and inventive.

There's an old story—true or not we cannot guarantee—about Edmund Burke delivering his now famous speech against Warren Hastings. At one point in the speech he suddenly stopped in the middle of an idea. Slowly and impressively he raised his hand and pointed his index finger at Mr. Hastings. He stood for almost a minute with that dramatic pointing finger while the audience almost held its breath. Then he went on.

Afterward, one of the opposing advocates said, "Mr. Burke, that was one of the most effective pauses I have ever seen. We in the audience simply held our breaths, wondering what you were going to say next."

"That," responded Mr. Burke, "is exactly the way I was feeling."

INDEX

V

W